THE POWER OF A CLEAR CONSCIENCE

ERWIN W. LUTZER

HARVEST HOUSE PUBLISHERS
EUGENE, OREGON

Cover by Dual Identity, Inc, Whites Creek , Tennessee

Cover photo © Baldas 1950 / Shutterstock

Some of the general thoughts presented in chapter 1, "Out of the Shadows," are also covered in chapter 1 of the author's book *Making the Best of a Bad Decision* (Carol Stream, IL: Tyndale House, 2011).

Portions of chapter 7, "Conflicts of Conscience," were adapted from pages 217-230 of the author's book *Who Are You to Judge?* (Chicago: Moody Publishers, 2003), and are used with permission.

THE POWER OF A CLEAR CONSCIENCE

Copyright © 2016 Erwin W. Lutzer
Published by Harvest House Publishers
Eugene, Oregon 97408
www.harvesthousepublishers.com

ISBN 978-0-7369-5305-4 (pbk.)
ISBN 978-0-7369-5307-8 (eBook)

Library of Congress Cataloging-in-Publication Data
Names: Lutzer, Erwin W., author.
Title: The power of a clear conscience / Erwin W. Lutzer.
Description: Eugene : Harvest House Publishers, 2016. | Includes
    bibliographical references.
Identifiers: LCCN 2016019285 (print) | LCCN 2016020786 (ebook) | ISBN
    9780736953054 (pbk.) | ISBN 9780736953078 ()
Subjects: LCSH: Conscience—Religious aspects—Christianity. |
    Guilt—Religious aspects—Christianity. | Forgiveness of sin.
Classification: LCC BJ1278.C66 L88 2016 (print) | LCC BJ1278.C66 (ebook) |
    DDC 241/.1—dc23
LC record available at https://lccn.loc.gov/2016019285

Printed in the United States of America

21 22 23 24 / BP-JC / 10 9 8 7 6 5 4 3

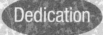

Dedication

This book is dedicated to all those whose conscience tells them that they have sinned too much to be forgiven, or those who think their past must define their future. These pages were written so that all might understand that when we have done our worst, grace stands by to do its best.

"Now the law came to increase the trespass, but where sin increased, grace abounded all the more, so that, as sin reigned in death, grace might reign through righteousness leading to eternal life through Jesus Christ our Lord" (Romans 5:20-21).

Contents

Out of the Shadow

*There is no witness so terrible and no accuser
so powerful as conscience which dwells within us.*

Sophocles

In *Hamlet,* Shakespeare wrote, "Conscience does make cowards of us all." How true! It doesn't matter what your background is, what religious tradition you were brought up in, or whether you were raised in a nonreligious home. I can assure you that you have at times violated your conscience. Our conscience sits in judgment on all of our actions and says, "Aha! You have violated what you know to be right."

In the book *The Holy War* by John Bunyan, there's a town called Mansoul (man's soul) that's taken over by Diabolos (the devil), who is the false prince. This evil ruler takes control over the city except for the town crier, namely Old Man, Conscience. Although Diabolos takes control, occasionally the town crier (Conscience) rings the bell and runs up and down the street saying, "Diabolos is a liar and a cheat! Prince Emmanuel is the true prince of Mansoul!" In other words, in a world of universal delusion it's the voice of Conscience that reminds people that there is a higher law to which all must yield. The Liar, Diabolos, doesn't have the last word.

In 1968, English businessman Donald Crowhurst veered off course in the *Golden Globe* yacht race around the world, but evidently attempted to steal victory by lying low on the coast of South America and waiting to rejoin his competitors when they circled back around. He sent false radio reports of his progress and might have fooled the world had not his deceit riddled him with guilt.

Crowhurst suspected that his hoax would be discovered, so he jumped overboard and drowned. He left his records intact, which exposed his deception so that all of the world could see that he had planned to win the race by cheating. It appeared as though he wanted to die, admitting to what he had done and clearing his conscience as best he could.

Our conscience has the power to bless us or condemn us; it can drive us to do great ventures for God, or it can lead us to anger, sleepless nights, and an unending cycle of despair. This internal voice will not be satisfied with our rationalizations.

What Is the Conscience?

What is the conscience? The word itself comes from two words: *con*, which means "with," and *science*, which means "knowledge." Conscience is "knowledge along with us," or more specifically, the knowledge we carry *within* us. The conscience is powerful, and in this opening chapter we're going to look at its origin and its implications for us.

There are three characteristics of the conscience that are important for our study.

First, *conscience is universal*. Every person has a conscience. In the New Testament, the apostle Paul argues that the Jews, who had the law of God and therefore knew His will, and the Gentiles, who did not have the written law, have both violated God's standards and stand guilty before Him. The Jews are convicted by God's law, Paul says, while the Gentiles will be judged by their conscience:

> When Gentiles, who do not have the law, by nature do
> what the law requires, they are a law to themselves, even
> though they do not have the law. They show that the
> work of the law is written on their hearts, while their
> conscience also bears witness, and their conflicting
> thoughts accuse or even excuse them on that day when,
> according to my gospel, God judges the secrets of men
> by Christ Jesus (Romans 2:14-16).

As for the Gentiles, their conscience is either going to accuse or excuse them. The conscience is the rudimentary law of God written on every human heart.

I spoke with a woman who said she was comfortable with atheism. If God was there, He wasn't there for her when she needed Him. Yet she did admit to guilt, twinges of regret, and the inner recognition that she had seriously misbehaved. She confessed some dirty laundry that she had to process and said she had no means to wipe her slate clean. "I know that when I face death," she said, "I will begin to worry if there is 'something on the other side.'"

Don't misunderstand. I'm not saying that everyone has the same standard of right and wrong. Rather, I am saying that everyone has a conscience that sits in judgment on their actions, even if the verdict of conscience sometimes differs from culture to culture and from home to home.

We've all gone through metal detectors at the airport; sometimes my belt buckle has set off the alarm, other times it hasn't. I'm told that machines can be tuned to be more sensitive or less sensitive. Just so, my conscience might be set at one reading and yours at another; my conscience might disapprove of an action that yours approves of. In minor matters, our inner judge might render a different verdict, but in the basics of morality, there is general agreement. And every individual has at times experienced that inner voice that tells him, "What you did wasn't right."

Even pagans have a conscience. This distinguishes us from animals; yes, animals can experience some sense of shame, depending on human conditioning, but there is no evidence that animals can actually be troubled by their own behavior. The lion is not bothered about depriving a mother deer of her fawn; the snake is not troubled by destroying the eggs of a bird; the bear is not troubled for mauling a child. One piece of evidence for the existence of God is that human beings, created in His image, live with an "ought" deep within.

Second, *conscience can be conditioned.* This feature of the human conscience can have both positive and negative effects. In an entirely different context, Paul talks about some Christians whose conscience prohibits them from doing something (such as eating meat that has been offered to idols), while other Christians' consciences give them the freedom to do so (see Romans 14:1-4, 10-12). In a future chapter, we shall discuss these differences in detail.

So although the conscience is not always an infallible guide, it either approves or disapproves of the basic moral decisions we make. Almost universally the conscience witnesses within us that stealing, lying, and sexual immorality are wrong.

Third, *conscience has tremendous power.* It can haunt us day and night, and eventually destroy us. Later on, we're going to talk about Lady Macbeth from Shakespeare's play, whose tormented conscience drove her to suicide. (The good news is that Lady Macbeth didn't have to commit suicide, and no one else does either.)

Here's our dilemma: Our conscience usually doesn't trouble us before we commit a particular act; it remains silent even when we contemplate wrongdoing. But afterward, especially as we lie down to sleep at night, it keeps interrupting our peace. I have little doubt that the reason sleeping pills are used so widely is because so many go to bed with a conscience that robs them of rest. Conscience can prevent us from falling asleep at night and it awakens us early in the morning. Sometimes it yells at us.

I'm friends with a Christian man whose mother checked into a psychiatric ward a number of times while he was growing up. When he was twenty-two, his mother confessed to him that the man he thought was his father wasn't his biological father after all. His father was actually a doctor in the community with whom she'd had an affair.

Imagine what this startling confession did to this young man. He struggled emotionally and spiritually, trying to come to terms with who he really was, and questioning his self-worth. After all, strictly speaking, he should not have been born.

Yet today he has an effective ministry and speaks in various churches with joy, challenging people to experience spiritual renewal. He is proof that your parental origin doesn't have to stop you from enjoying a blessed life and making a positive impact. The key is to take advantage of the marvelous, incredible grace of God.

We shouldn't be surprised that after his mother confessed her years of deception, she didn't have to return to the psychiatric ward. At last she was at peace. I remember reading the words of a doctor who said, "I could dismiss half of my patients if I could just look them in the eye and give them the assurance that they are forgiven."

The eminent psychiatrist Karl Menninger wrote a famous book entitled *Whatever Became of Sin?* in which he said:

The very word, "sin," which seems to have disappeared, was a proud word. It was once a strong word, an ominous and serious word. But the word went away. It has almost disappeared—the word, along with the notion. Why? Doesn't anyone sin anymore? Doesn't anyone believe in sin?[1]

Dr. Menninger was arguing that mental health and moral health are inseparably linked, so he insisted that agents of moral teaching—such as educators and parents—are just as necessary to a person's well-being as the psychiatrist. Of course, as we shall learn, ultimately, only God can clear our conscience.

There is a man who is a wonderful Christian with a lovely wife and children. But every time he was asked to be an elder in his church, he said no. He was asked, "Why? You are gifted. You know the Bible."

But years later, he confessed to his pastor that when he was in college, he'd had an affair with a young woman who had his child, who was now growing up in another city. He knew he was forgiven by God, but because he kept this secret from his wife, he was always haunted by his past. Spiritually and mentally, he was unable to get beyond his past. He knew that his silence was deception, and he also knew that one day his son might appear at his front door. No matter how often he justified his silence, the fact of his son was always present in his mind. (In a future chapter, we will discuss the topic of reconciliation with others.)

In the book of Acts, the early disciples were characterized as having joy and gladness (see 2:46). The primary reason for their joy was because they had experienced forgiveness that had freed them from condemnation. The apostle John beautifully expressed this joy and freedom: "Beloved, if our heart does not condemn us, we have confidence before God" (1 John 3:21). If we have a condemning conscience, we can still believe, but not with very much "confidence before God."

The purpose of this book is to help you live with the confidence that comes from a conscience that is clear before God and before others. Someone has said that we are all either in denial or in recovery! Hopefully in these pages our denial will be exposed and we will move on to recovery.

The Origin of the Conscience

Let's go back to the beginning. In the Garden of Eden, Adam and Eve had a perfect environment: They had all the beauty, all the food, and all the other comforts of life they could ever want.

What is more, they had fellowship with God, who came walking with them "in the cool of the day" (Genesis 3:8). Theologians use the word *innocence* to describe this couple before sin entered the world. Think of the joy they had: Eve had no insecurities. She didn't have to compete with the supermodels whose faces appeared on the newsstands or in the checkout line at the grocery store. She didn't even have to lie awake at night wondering if she had married the right man! And yet, for all of that, she and Adam decided to sin. Here is the tragic story:

> Now the serpent was more crafty than any other beast of the field that the LORD God had made. He said to the woman, "Did God actually say, 'You shall not eat of any tree in the garden'?" And the woman said to the serpent, "We may eat of the fruit of the trees in the garden, but God said, 'You shall not eat of the fruit of the tree that is in the midst of the garden, neither shall you touch it, lest you die.'" But the serpent said to the woman, "You will not surely die. For God knows that when you eat of it your eyes will be opened, and you will be like God, knowing good and evil" (Genesis 3:1-5).

The serpent promised Adam and Eve that if they chose to be their own god, they could make independent decisions about right and wrong. The serpent was, in effect, saying to Eve, "*Feel*, don't think. Don't you see that the fruit is beautiful?" We know Adam was standing next to her, for when she offered the forbidden fruit to him, he also ate with her (verse 6). Quite possibly the first sin might have been Adam abdicating his responsibility as a husband; he didn't stop his wife from disobeying God's command. Instead, he actually participated with her.

The unintended consequences were not long in coming. They could not have predicted the fallout. God had said, "In the day that you eat of it you shall surely die" (Genesis 2:17). Adam and

Eve had no experience of death, so they thought they could handle whatever consequences would ensue. Furthermore, if they didn't eat, they would always wonder what it would have been like; curiosity would have spawned the regret of not risking disobedience.

What the couple didn't know was that they had just toppled the first in a long line of dominoes that are still falling today. They could never have predicted that someday they would have a son by the name of Cain who would kill his brother, Abel. Evil would now enter the human race and zigzag throughout history, bringing destruction with it.

They couldn't predict the consequences of their sin, and neither can we predict the consequences of our own. Like a basketball we attempt to submerge in the ocean, we might think we have hidden our mess, but then it bobbles up somewhere else. The unintended consequences bedevil us!

The Entrance of Shame

Before they sinned, Adam and Eve didn't need the voice of conscience because they were without guilt. We read, "The man and his wife were both naked and were not ashamed" (Genesis 2:25).

But when sin entered into their lives, everything changed. Their conscience now condemned them.

> They heard the sound of the Lord God walking in the garden in the cool of the day, and the man and his wife hid themselves from the presence of the Lord God among the trees of the garden. But the Lord God called to the man and said to him, "Where are you?" And he said, "I heard the sound of you in the garden, and I was afraid, because I was naked, and I hid myself." He said, "Who told you that you were naked?" (3:8-11).

Who told them that they were naked? No other human being was lurking in the shadows telling them that they had sinned. No bird in a tree chirped the news. Their own awakened *conscience told them they had sinned and had reason to feel shame.*

Every human being would now have similar experiences. Many children would now be reared in a shame-based home: they would not only grow up feeling ashamed for their own sin but also be afflicted by the sin and shame of their parents.

I've titled the next chapter "It's Not All Your Fault" because we often inherit the shame or guilt of our parents. Poverty, alcoholism and addictions, brokenness, and abuse all impose shame on the life of a child. The implications can be devastating.

Adam and Eve's shame led them to hiding. They hid from God and from one another. They tried to manage their sin by putting their guilt into one compartment of their lives and use their minds to either justify their disobedience or suppress their persistent conscience. They now had a hidden life and a public life; the hidden life must not be seen by anyone lest their shame be revealed.

All of us have a private life we don't want others to see. I recall a statement made by the venerable J. Vernon McGee, speaking from the platform of The Moody Church during Moody Bible Institute's annual Bible Conference. He said in his gravelly voice, "If you knew my heart the way I know my heart, you wouldn't listen to me." Then he paused and said, "Now before you run to the exits, if I knew your heart the way you know your heart, I wouldn't even be talking to you."

The sin in the hidden part of our lives can grow to become an addiction, or even lead to criminal behavior. Here's a scenario that's happened many times: In compartment A, Mr. Smith is a Sunday school teacher. He is well thought of. He is respected in the community and in his church. But in compartment B, Mr. Smith is an abuser at home. He's an alcoholic. He's an addict. He has learned to manage his sin and put on a righteous façade. At all costs, his sin and shame must be hidden.

It's like men who want to erase everything from the hard drive of their computer so that they can present a clean image to others; they don't want anyone to see what they've been viewing. Shame must be covered.

My point is simply that the sin of Adam and Eve has affected all of us; we have all been born in sin (see Psalm 51:5). Only honesty before God, and often before others, clears our conscience.

More on that later.

Shame Leads to Blame

Adam played the "blame card" as soon as God confronted him. Adam was hiding, so God asked him: "Who told you that you were naked? Have you eaten of the tree of which I commanded you not to eat?" (Genesis 3:11). He had a ready answer: "The woman whom you gave to be with me, she gave me the fruit of the tree, and I ate." It's the *woman's* fault!

Let me paraphrase Adam's response. "Lord, this is really *Your* fault! This weak-willed woman whom *You* gave me ate of the fruit and offered it to me. What was I to do? *She* is to blame." Notice that Adam blamed his wife even though there wasn't a chance in the world that he had married the wrong woman!

Now it was Eve's turn to shift blame. "Then the LORD God said to the woman, 'What is this that you have done?' The woman said, "The serpent deceived me, and I ate'" (Genesis 3:13).

Someone has said, "So the man blamed the woman, the woman blamed the serpent—and the serpent didn't have a leg to stand on!" As humorist Will Rogers said, "There are two eras in American history—the passing of the buffalo and the passing of the buck."

History constantly repeats itself. As soon as sin is exposed, the blaming begins. "It's *his* fault." "It's *her* fault." "It's the *kid's* fault." "It's *my employer's* fault." People are going to defend themselves at any cost. If need be, they will come to a confrontation with a pack of lies, ready to justify themselves.

In the novel *The Fall,* the famed French secular philosopher Albert Camus said, "Each of us insists on being innocent at all cost, even if he has to accuse the whole human race and heaven itself."[2]

We will dig in our heels. If we need to lie, we'll lie. If we can't lie, we'll tweak the truth. We'll shift the blame because we have to hide our true selves from others, even from ourselves, and yes, even from God, if that were possible.

But the conscience does not forget, and it will not be silenced. Even when we think we have successfully suppressed it, it shows up at unexpected times.

No Return to Innocence

Innocence once lost cannot be regained. Adam and Eve were barred from returning to Eden. Nor can we return to the days of our innocence. A girl who has lost her virginity cannot get it back. A man who has abandoned his family and forced his children to grow up fatherless cannot undo his selfish choices. We can't pray like the teenager, "Oh God, I pray that this accident might not have happened." The past is past, there is no returning to Eden.

Everything changed for Adam and Eve. No sooner had they eaten the forbidden fruit than "the eyes of both were opened, and they knew that they were naked. And they sewed fig leaves together and made themselves loincloths" (Genesis 3:7).

What Satan said was partially true. Their eyes were opened to the reality of their nakedness. So to cover their shame, they made a covering of fig leaves. Ever since, we have all sewn our own fig leaves to hide our true selves and cover our shame. We are thinking, *No one is ever going to see me as inadequate; no one will ever see me as I really am. No one will see my shame.*

For some, the fig leaves are quite literally beautiful clothes; for others, it's a beautiful body. For still others it's becoming a success in business, willing to trample on others to get where they want to go. So whether it's money, fame, sex, or a combination of all three, people have been willing to destroy their families, become deceptive, and in short, do whatever they think is needed to gain significance.

Meanwhile, behind the appearance of success is deep-seated inadequacy, shame, and a restless conscience. The fig leaves don't cover all the hidden parts. The empty rot within just won't go away. And yet the mask must be held firmly in place.

"Just worship me and we'll get along fine!" read the lettering on a T-shirt. But left to ourselves, we not only want worship, we want to outdo any rival gods. We have to look better than the person next to us.

When the fig leaves don't hide the inner despair and guilt, people turn to alcoholism, drugs, and sex. And in their disillusionment, they just might end up a victim of suicide.

God's Healing for a Damaged Conscience

Aren't you glad that Adam and Eve's story, and ours, doesn't end with fig leaves? God intervened on behalf of our first parents, and He intervenes for us as well.

God went looking for Adam and Eve. Notice that they weren't looking for Him. They weren't saying, "Where can we find God? Let's run to Him and see if we can restore our fellowship with Him."

No, they hid from God and so do we. The New Testament confirms that "no one seeks for God...not even one" (Romans 3:11-12). You say, "Well, I sought after God." But the reality is that God took the initiative and began a search for you and found you. He came looking for you. In John 15:16, Jesus said, "You did not choose me, but I chose you."

God came to the Garden with some clothes so that Adam and Eve didn't have to wrestle with guilt and haunting shame. "The LORD God made for Adam and for his wife garments of skins and clothed them" (3:21). Where did God get the garments of skin? Obviously He killed some of the animals He had created. What God was saying right at the beginning was that *there is no cheap covering for sin.*

Our fig leaves might improve our appearance for others, but they don't hide us from God. But with God's wardrobe, we can live with a conscience that no longer condemns us. The blood that was shed to kill the animals that supplied clothes for Adam and Eve pointed forward to the once-for-all sacrifice of Jesus Christ, who shed His blood on our behalf. This is God's answer for our sin—and it isn't cheap. Our sin can be covered, but not by us.

As Adam and Eve discovered, the consequences of sin are messy, but our guilt is not the last word. Back when I was a boy, we spilled some oil on the concrete floor in our garage, and couldn't get rid of the stain. Therefore, if we wanted to do work on that concrete, we had to put a tarp over the mess. As far as we were concerned, the oil spill had never happened.

Beginning with this first blood sacrifice for sin in Genesis 3, God would go on to work more deeply in the human heart so that we would not just be legally forgiven, but our hearts would actually be cleansed. Sin wouldn't just be covered, but even better, it would be taken away.

And that leads to the topic of this book: *God is able to take our past and cover it, and then cleanse our conscience.* He has made it possible for us to not only be forgiven, but to approach Him with a clear conscience.

The accusations can stop. We can sleep at night when we're in fellowship with God, and to the extent possible, in fellowship with others. There's enough grace in God's heart for the sins of our past.

The Continuing Consequences

Yes, Adam and Eve's sin was forgiven. They were back in fellowship with God, but nothing was the same. Standing there with their new clothes, they might have had an argument:

Adam says, "Well, you did it first."

"Yeah, but you were standing next to me."

"Okay, sure I was standing there, but who actually took the first bite? Who's going to clean up this mess?"

"Don't look at me! Look at yourself, Adam. Didn't God say you're supposed to be the head of our home? He's going to hold you responsible. You were standing right beside me. Why didn't you say something?"

Eve is right; God does hold Adam responsible. But she can't escape responsibility either. There's plenty of blame to go around. We can imagine that the arguments continued when they were stuck with Cain, a problem child who killed Abel, his younger brother.

And so, very rapidly, the whole history of the human race fell apart as evil had its way. You and I today are caught in this same vortex of evil desires within us and temptations around us. We are born with a sin nature and come into this world under God's condemnation. We feel the sting of guilt for what we have done and for what we have not done. There is even the shame of what others have done to us.

God was gracious in preventing Adam and Eve from returning to Eden. If they had gone back and eaten of the fruit of the tree of life, they would have lived forever as sinners.

God had a better plan.

Jesus would be sent to fully redeem us: body, soul, and spirit. Sin would win many victories, but it would lose the war. Because of Jesus' sacrifice, we can be eternally forgiven in this life. Then at death, our spirit will go to be with God, and at a later time, our bodies will be raised. An unimaginable heaven is being prepared for all who trust in God's Redeemer.

The issue before us is not the greatness of our sin—even if we think we have committed the greatest sin imaginable. "Where sin increased, grace abounded all the more" (Romans 5:20). Grace is a game-changer. Sin loses its power in the presence of God's super-abounding grace.

Recently I read a remarkable book about a US Army chaplain named Henry Gerecke. He was a Lutheran pastor who joined the army during World War II. Because he spoke German, he found himself serving as chaplain to the cruel Nazi leaders who were on trial in Nuremberg, Germany, for their horrible war crimes. Incredibly, at least five of these men (and perhaps seven), most of whom were hanged for their crimes, came to saving faith in Jesus Christ as a result of the faithful witness of Chaplain Gerecke.[3]

Grace isn't fair! I thought as I read these stories of redemption. But the long arm of grace reaches out to people who clearly don't deserve it. It reaches out to those who deserve hell; it reaches out to all of us!

"Blessed is the one whose transgression is forgiven, whose sin is covered. Blessed is the man against whom the LORD counts no iniquity, and in whose spirit there is no deceit" (Psalm 32:1-2).

Your conscience can be legally silenced. Let your invisible accuser drive you toward God and not away from Him. Let God find you.

Your past is not the final word.

A Passage to Ponder:

Blessed is the one whose transgression is forgiven,
   whose sin is covered.
Blessed is the man against whom the LORD
   counts no iniquity,
      and in whose spirit there is no deceit
      (Psalm 32:1-2).

Probing Questions to Consider:

Why do you think God allowed Adam and Eve the opportunity to sin? Think of decisions you have made that had unintended consequences. Were you able to enjoy God's forgiveness despite the fallout?

What fig leaves do we wear to cover our shame and guilt?

Pause to thank God for providing a permanent covering for our sin.

It's Not All Your Fault

All peace inwardly and peace outwardly is
based on this vertical experience of:
Do I have peace with God? Is it open and
clear with God? Are we friends?[1]

JOHN PIPER

Let's imagine we're sitting at a table enjoying a cup of coffee (or do you prefer tea?). Let's suppose you're struggling with guilt and shame for something you've done, but you're also telling me about your abusive family background. Clearly, bad parenting has affected your life, and the consequences just keep piling up.

Here's my desire for you: "The aim of our charge [or instruction] is love that issues from a pure heart and a good conscience and a sincere faith" (1 Timothy 1:5). Simply put, without a pure heart, you can't have a good conscience. And without a good conscience and a pure heart, you really can't give or receive love. These three qualities—love, faith, and a good conscience—are intimately connected.

Let's assume you were brought up with an abusive, alcoholic father, and an indifferent, passive mother who covered for your dad, enabling him to get by with his lies, excuses, and abuse. Or your situation may have been different, but the bottom line is still the same: You grew up in a home where you had family secrets, where no one was allowed to talk honestly about their pain, their fears, and their abuse, no matter what form it took. Shame was always covered superficially.

The purpose of this chapter is to help you lay down your emotional backpack of guilt, shame, and anger. Or at least to help you to continue your journey with a lighter load, taking steps toward a "good conscience" without the past constantly blocking your path to pursue a more fulfilling future.

Some counselors distinguish between guilt and shame, but I'm going to use the words interchangeably for now. I think of shame as a subset of guilt. Or we could just say that I'm speaking about guilt-laden baggage from your past, however it may be defined.

Secondhand Guilt

Here's a bit of good news: *It's not all your fault!* Some of the guilt you carry may be of your doing, but not all of it. Children often inherit shame and guilt, particularly from their parents. One generation passes their baggage on to another, and the cycle continues.

Here are some examples.

Abusive Parents

Let's return to those harsh, uncaring parents who devalued you. One time, while I was in a supermarket, I saw a mother yank her child and shout, "Why are you so stupid? Don't you know how to behave?" If she does that in public, imagine what goes on when the child gets home. Broken families generate anger, and uncontrolled anger leads to abuse—and abuse leads to shame.

The whole world got upset when a famous football player knocked his girlfriend unconscious in an elevator. That inexcusable act of abuse was caught on security cameras, but I'm afraid that if hidden cameras were set up in our own homes, we'd discover that abuse exists almost everywhere behind closed doors, and often-times even in church families. Unfortunately, what that football player had done isn't unusual.

My wife, Rebecca, and I were driving into Chicago one morn-ing when I said to her, "I wonder how much abuse took place in this city last night or this morning?" It's all around us, and if you were a victim, you have, no doubt, inherited the debilitating shame and guilt that comes with it and whispers, "You are worthless." Or perhaps even, "Every awful thing that has happened to you is your fault."

Abuse is largely responsible for an epidemic of shame that exists in our world.

Addictive Parents

I don't want to overemphasize the role of bad parenting, but I have to put addictive parents in their own category. Addictive par-ents are manipulative, often making their children tell lies to cover up family secrets. Addictive parents use their children for their (the parents') own ends. Even as they grow older, addictive parents con-tinue to motivate their children through guilt, excuses, and blam-ing others for whatever "bad luck" they have experienced.

One woman, brought up with a controlling, guilt-motivating mother, said, "My mother must have the whole Midwest franchise for guilt distribution." Can't you just hear her mother? "After all, didn't we raise you? Don't you owe it to us to be loving and let us enjoy our grandchildren? And by the way, I also need some money." Yes, that woman had enough guilt for herself, but also for anyone she aspired to control. Her daughter had to set boundaries and no longer be a puppet as she responded to her mother's emotional and financial expectations.

Yes, boundaries are necessary. One man said to me, "When-ever my mother-in-law comes for a visit, she destroys our family relationships. She tries to drive a wedge between me and my wife, and even criticizes us with the children present." My response: "Be loving, but firm. Your responsibility is to protect both your wife and your children." *Guess what, Grandma; you are no longer welcome in our home.*

We have to own our own stuff. But we don't have to accept the guilt and shame inherited from insensitive, controlling, and self-serving parents—or grandparents.

Honest Mistakes

False guilt can take many forms. Sometimes we feel guilty for honest mistakes. False guilt is subjective guilt and refers to acquired guilt that we don't deserve; whereas objective guilt means that we're guilty for something we've actually done. False guilt is often difficult to identify and admit to.

My parents knew a woman who convinced her husband to go to a concert. He reluctantly went with her, and that evening they were involved in a car accident in which he was killed. For thirteen years, that woman made regular trips to his grave, heaping upon herself all the responsibility and the guilt for having convinced her husband to go to the concert with her.

I wish I could have said to this woman, "God does not want you to feel guilty for something you did with the best of intentions." All of us have convinced our mates to go somewhere they didn't want to go, and tragedy could have befallen any of us.

And then I think of the mother whose little girl said, "Mommy, can I cross the street?" The mother, seeing no vehicle, thoughtlessly said *yes.* The little girl darted into the street and was killed by a car.

No parent ever gets over such a tragedy. But be assured that God does not lay guilt on us for a tragic mistake. There comes a time when we must simply accept what has happened and, as best as we can, move on. As the late Elisabeth Elliot said, "In acceptance lies peace."

God wants us to have a good conscience, and He stands ready to help us move beyond the guilt, shame, and regret that isn't our fault. He understands. He knows. He cares.

Shame from Sexual Exploitation

Now let me comment on the most powerful kind of unde-served shame—it is the shame carried by victims of sexual exploi-tation. I want to illustrate this from a truly tragic story in 2 Samuel 13:1-22, involving King David's daughter Tamar, her half-brother Amnon, and her full brother Absalom.

David had multiple wives, so there were a variety of relation-ships within his dysfunctional family. Tamar was a very beautiful virgin, and her half-brother Amnon was filled with burning lust for her. Indeed, the Bible says that "Amnon was so tormented [by his lust] that he made himself ill because of his sister Tamar, for she was a virgin, and it seemed impossible to Amnon to do anything to her" (2 Samuel 13:2).

The Despicable Act

But Amnon had a friend named Jonadab who was very "crafty" (verse 3). Jonadab noticed Amnon moping around day after day and asked him what was bothering him. Amnon told him of his lustful desire for Tamar, and Jonadab hatched a plan that went something like this: "Why don't you pretend that you're sick, and ask your father, King David, to send Tamar to you with food? Then when you're alone together in your bedroom, you can do whatever you like" (see verse 5). What Jonadab meant was, "You can over-power her and sexually assault her."

The plan sounded good to Amnon. As he pretended to be sick, his father David came to see him, and Amnon made his evil request (verse 6). David agreed and foolishly said to Tamar, "Go to your brother Amnon's house and prepare food for him" (verse 7).

Tamar obeyed David, and when she was alone with Amnon, he said, "Come, lie with me, my sister" (verse 11). She answered, "No, my brother, do not violate me, for such a thing is not done in Israel; do not do this outrageous thing" (verse 12). But Tamar's plea fell on deaf ears as Amnon assaulted her sexually.

All-Consuming Shame

One of the tragedies of sexual exploitation is that the victims' cries for help are not heard by their abusers. Tamar's anguished question, "Where could I carry my shame?" (verse 13), brings tears to our eyes. Where would she put this shame? How would she be able to carry this heavy emotional load, the stigma of a defiled woman?

Amnon raped his half-sister with no concern for her. And it only got worse. After his crime, "[Amnon] hated her with very great hatred, so that the hatred with which he hated her was greater than the love with which he had loved her" (verse 15). In sexual abuse, hate and lust often go hand in hand.

Tamar was put out of the room and the door was bolted behind her. She had been personally violated and was now utterly humiliated. She expressed her desolation according to the custom of that day by putting ashes on her head, tearing the "long robe" she was wearing (which, by the way, was a sign of her lost virginity) and crying loudly as she ran away (verse 19).

Perhaps the saddest part of this story is that this crime defined the rest of her life. We read that "Tamar lived, a desolate woman, in her brother Absalom's house" (verse 20). This innocent woman was ruined by shame, not because of what she did, but because of what someone else did to her. She had been defiled by a wicked, self-serving man. Now her life was ruined by hatred and shame.

What did her father, David, do when he heard about this evil? The answer is *nothing*. "When King David heard of all these things, he was very angry" (verse 21). Why didn't he step in to defend

Tamar and bring Amnon to justice? He got angry, yes, but like all passive fathers, he did nothing.

I think I know why. Just two chapters earlier, in 2 Samuel 11, we read that David committed adultery with Bathsheba and murdered her husband Uriah to cover the deed. With that, David lost all moral authority within his family. Thus he became the typical passive father who gets angry with his children but has no meaningful involvement in their lives. The passive father has his own load of guilt and shame and doesn't know how to control his dysfunctional family. Rather than dealing with his own issues to try to regain his authority, he just looks the other way.

The world is full of young women (and men) who, like Tamar, have been used and abused and carry with them the stigma of someone else's abuse.

Consequences of Guilt and Shame

Those who have inherited shame because of evil done against them can quickly turn to various forms of destructive behavior. What are some ways that the victims of imposed guilt and shame manage the conflict within their own hearts?

The Destruction of Self-Worth

Sadly, victims of abuse often marry an abuser. There is bonding to abuse; the victim feels that he or she deserves to be abused. If they're not being abused, they're not getting what they deserve. Instead of laying the blame where it belongs, many abused children are made to feel so defiled and unworthy that they come to believe they *deserve* the abuse.

Remember, abusers are also master manipulators. They say things like, "If you weren't such a bad wife, I wouldn't have to hit you!" Or, "If you tell anyone what I've done, you'll destroy our family, and I'll see to it that you get the blame."

Let children be berated often enough, and they'll come to believe the warnings and accusations. They'll become addicted to failure, addicted to being abused. They'll expect to fail in life and develop a sense of "learned helplessness." Even if such victims have the opportunity to change or to leave the abusive situation, many do not.

Here is where healthy families have to step in to give such children hope and the assurance that their future can be different than their past. The victims have to be validated; they need to see that they are worthy, they need affirmation and the acceptance of others, and above all, the assurance that God has welcomed them into His family.

Compulsive Behaviors

Another very unhealthy way to deal with undeserved guilt and shame is through compulsive behaviors. For example, there are people who wash their hands or take a bath many times a day because it gives them a bit of relief from feeling dirty or feeling responsible for their inadequacy. Others, particularly children and teenagers, inflict pain on themselves because they feel so worthless they think they deserve to suffer. They feel guilty simply for being alive. They have been belittled and devalued by their upbringing or by their relationships as Tamar was. Thus they slash their wrists and feel better for a few moments, thinking that their own blood will "even the score" and ease their troubled conscience and their sense of worthlessness.

Perfectionists fear being exposed or being seen as inadequate. They fear being naked, figuratively speaking. So they demand perfection of themselves and everyone around them. They develop a low-grade anger toward themselves because they don't live up to their own expectations. And they also become angry with others who fall far beneath their impossible standards. Thus they're unhappy with everyone and everything, but keep pushing for perfection as the cycle of failed expectations and the anger that follows goes on and on. They fear being shamed, so they work hard to keep the doors of their lives private and hidden behind work, money, sex, alcoholism, or drugs.

We are familiar with extreme examples of paranoia. But there is also a hidden aspect of paranoia that often occurs in the most natural relationships. The paranoid person is saying to himself, "I expect to be betrayed, and if you criticize me, I assume that you are an enemy whose intention is to betray me. You are in cahoots with all those other people who are out to destroy me."

Such responses are the result of a great feeling of inadequacy, a feeling of internal insecurity, a great fear of being exposed and found to be deserving of shame.

Paranoia is a form of denial. People develop false worlds in which they are the heroes and everyone else is their enemy. The building of defenses is carefully crafted to keep others at bay so they won't discover the person behind the mask.

Control freaks are often filled with inner feelings of shame and inadequacy. They are convinced that if they can control their environment and everyone in it, they'll never have to feel guilty or be shamed again. But few people appreciate being controlled, so this frustrates the controller. Meanwhile their own conscience is not at rest, and they become victims of their own inadequacy even as they are constantly critical of others for their failures.

God to the Rescue

Enough of analysis. Let us invite God into this picture so He can give us the hope we all seek. Here are three statements of encouragement that you need to remember.

Beauty Replaces Shame

Let us return to Tamar.

She put ashes on her head as a sign of her perpetual mourning. But to the nation Israel, God makes a promise of restoration, which I believe can be applied to us.

God promises beauty in the place of ashes. "To grant to those who mourn in Zion—to give them a beautiful headdress instead of ashes, the oil of gladness instead of mourning, the garment of praise instead of a faint spirit; that they may be called oaks of righteousness, the planting of the LORD, that he may be glorified" (Isaiah 61:3).

The Hebrew text teaches that the humiliating ashes can be replaced by a beautiful headdress. The shame of mourning can be removed. The inherited stigma need no longer define the victim.

God is willing to put your shame away and replace it with the beauty of His love and forgiveness. And Isaiah goes on to say, "You shall be called the priests of the LORD; they shall speak of you as the ministers of our God...Instead of your shame there shall be a double portion; instead of dishonor they shall rejoice in their lot" (verses 6-7).

And then finally we read in verse 10, "I will greatly rejoice in the LORD; my soul shall exult in my God, for he has clothed me with the garments of salvation."

The bottom line: God desires to give us dignity and acceptance in the place of our shame. He, not our parents, nor we ourselves, defines who we are.

Grace Replaces Guilt

God knows your need. He knows the objective shame you carry because of your sins. He also knows the subjective, undeserved shame you carry from your past.

No matter what the source of your shame and guilt may be,

God is bigger than all of it. In His grace and mercy, He can meet you in your need so that you have a "good conscience and a sincere faith."

In the New Testament, we have an even clearer understanding of God's cure for shame—the cross of Christ.

> Since we are surrounded by so great a cloud of witnesses, let us also lay aside every weight, and sin which clings so closely, and let us run with endurance the race that is set before us, looking to Jesus, the founder and perfecter of our faith, who for the joy that was set before him endured the cross, despising the *shame*, and is seated at the right hand of the throne of God (Hebrews 12:1-2, emphasis added).

The writer's point: When Jesus died on the cross, He scorned the shame connected with such a humiliating death. Hanging there was a shameful experience. He knew, in fact, that He was being cursed as He bore our sins because "cursed is everyone who is hanged on a tree" (Galatians 3:13; see also Deuteronomy 21:23).

The cross of Christ points us in the direction of hope.

Acceptance Replaces Shame

When Jesus was bearing our guilt on the cross, He was also bearing our shame. He was bringing about a deliverance that would go deep into our hearts so that we would be free. We can lay down our heavy emotional load on His shoulders.

I spoke with a woman who told me how, especially in church, she walked around with this heavy weight of shame that made it hard for her to see herself as a worthy person, much less as a daughter of God. But then as God began to lift the shame, she began to realize that she could walk around (and I encouraged her to do so) with her head held high, someone for whom shame is not the last word.

Author Rodney Clapp wrote these words about Hebrews 12:1-2 and the way Jesus has taken away our shame:

> Does shame bind us? Jesus was bound.
>
> Does shame destroy our reputation? Well, He was despised and rejected of men.
>
> Does shame reduce us to silence? He was led as a lamb to the slaughter and a sheep before its shearers is silent, so He opened not His mouth.
>
> Does shame expose our apparent weaknesses? "He saved others," the crowd mocked, "Himself He cannot save."
>
> Does shame lead to abandonment? Well, you think of the words of Jesus Christ on the cross. He said, "My God, My God, why hast Thou forsaken Me?"
>
> Does shame diminish us? He was crucified naked, exposed for gawkers to see. He bore our sins. He bore our iniquities. He bore the weight of our guilt, and the weight of our shame."[2]

The bottom line: Shame loses its power at the foot of the cross. Figuratively speaking, we can stoop to leave it there. At the cross, we are accepted and welcomed into fellowship with God.

There is no substitute for personal contact with God through Christ. Take all the shame, the guilt, and the fear in your heart and bring it to God. You need your dignity restored; you need to walk with your head held high as a son or daughter of God. It begins by realizing that your sin is put away from you and the past really is *past*.

Of course (and we will get into this later), you will also have to forgive those who have done wrong against you, even as Christ has forgiven you. "Be kind to one another, tenderhearted, forgiving one another, as God in Christ forgave you" (Ephesians 4:32).

You can forgive people even if you can no longer be reconciled to them. Perhaps your parents are dead, or your abuser would never admit to his evil ways and instead scorn you. There must come a time when you submit your anger and shame and resentment to God.

I've been told of a woman who took a train to another state, where her mother was buried, so she could stand at her grave and simply let all the hurt, anger, and shame spill out. Her mother had been a prostitute, so you can imagine the years of demoralizing painful experiences she had while growing up. Yet standing there at her mother's grave she said to God, "I give the shame and disgrace to you. I can't bear it anymore." This was an important step in the right direction.

That was not the end of her story. Her past would still well up in her mind, and all the old emotions would return. But now she knew what to do—namely, to keep giving her feelings to God and refusing to let them define who she was. Eventually the past loses its power.

Let God Redeem Your Story

Not only does shame lose its power at the foot of the cross; standing before God, you realize your self-worth is not based on how you feel. What God says about you in the Bible is much more important (and more true) than what your feelings tell you. He calls you by name and restores your dignity.

There is a frequently used illustration that helps us understand a proper sense of self-worth. If a silver dollar were found in a gutter all covered with smudge, it would be worth just as much as a shiny new silver dollar that had just been produced by the US Mint.

You may have been pushed into a moral cesspool or deliberately fell into one on your own accord. But your value as a person remains unchanged. God removes the smudge and confers His honor upon you. In His presence there is restored dignity and self-worth.

I have a friend who got involved in an adulterous relationship.

He eventually divorced his wife, and his children became estranged from him. His tears couldn't restore the broken relationships; he couldn't return to the way things once were. Every morning he woke up hoping that his wrecked life was a dream that would end.

Years later, I was riding with him in his car as he rehearsed his tale of self-made woes. Tears welled up in his eyes as he put a disc into his CD player, with a song sung by Dave Boyer, a well-known Christian artist who had been a nightclub singer before his conversion. Boyer's signature song is the old hymn "Calvary Covers It All."

In the song, Boyer proclaims the marvelous truth that at the cross, Jesus took our every sin, our every wrong, our every reason for guilt, and covered it all. There's another song that communicates this same truth with these words:

> My sin, oh the bliss of this glorious thought!
> My sin, not in part, but the whole,
> Is nailed to the cross, and I bear it no more,
> Praise the Lord, praise the Lord, O my soul![3]

The good news is that Jesus anticipated your sin and mine—our mess, our dysfunction, our guilt, and our shame. Jesus anticipated it all and in effect says to us, "When I died, I despised and scorned the shame of the cross. And I'll bear your shame if you'll believe on Me."

Moving beyond shame might be a gradual process, but the journey is well worth it. But it can only be done in the presence of God, along with the encouragement and support of other believers. I can't say it often enough: Emotional healing takes place best in the context of acceptance and love. The body of Christ, when it's functioning properly, is designed for self-healing. Isolation breeds despair, depression, and the continual fixation on shame, guilt, and anger. Love is the best healer.

Some emotional scars won't heal until we get to heaven. We may never entirely overcome our past, but God doesn't limit Himself to people from good homes and with healthy egos. Many people who were born into shame-based homes with addictions, abuse, and moral confusion have gone beyond their past to become successful. With a cleared conscience, they have believed that they could be all that God had ever intended.

God knows the shame you have brought on yourself and the shame others have imposed upon you. Either way, claim this promise: "The aim of our charge is love that issues from a pure heart and a *good conscience* and a sincere faith" (1 Timothy 1:5, emphasis added).

That is the goal of this book.

A Passage to Ponder:

Fear not, for you will not be ashamed; be not confounded, for you will not be disgraced; for you will forget the shame of your youth, and the reproach of your widowhood you will remember no more. For your Maker is your husband, the LORD of hosts is his name; and the Holy One of Israel is your Redeemer, the God of the whole earth he is called (Isaiah 54:4-5).

Probing Questions to Consider:

What has happened in your life that has caused shame or guilt? Submit these matters to God, one by one, and thank Jesus that He bore your shame.

Has your own struggle with guilt and shame affected those who are close to you? Take your time to answer that question in the presence of God, and consider how having a clear conscience would positively impact your relationships with others.

The Voice of God or
the Voice of the Devil

A condemning conscience is the devil's playground.

ERWIN LUTZER

Some people hear voices that say they should kill a neighbor who offended them, or dismember a child, or even kill themselves. They're haunted by voices that tell them to do what is despicable, but they think that they must do these evil deeds or they'd be disobeying God. We've all heard stories about criminals claiming to be obeying an inner compulsion of conscience.

And then there are those—often sincere Christians—who keep confessing the same sin over and over because they think that the accusations they feel are coming from God, not realizing that the feeling of continual condemnation is, in point of fact, coming from Satan, the one the Bible calls, "the accuser of our brethren" (Revelation 12:10 NASB). The result is perpetual guilt and unresolved condemnation. A clear conscience seems beyond reach for such people.

To unravel these issues, let's begin with a story from the Old Testament. Put yourself in the shoes of a man named Joshua, a high priest who stood guilty in the presence of God.

The prophet Zechariah had a vision that describes both our dilemma and God's answer to our guilt. In the vision, Joshua stood before God with shame, but then walked away declared as righteous as God Himself! His story can be our story. Satan was the accuser, and God was the one who sent the man away, acquitted.

Smudge on Our Clothes

Read carefully: "Then he showed me Joshua the high priest standing before the angel of the LORD, and Satan standing at his right hand to accuse him" (Zechariah 3:1). Visualize the scene: Joshua the priest (no relationship to Joshua the warrior, who has a book of the Old Testament named after him) represents all of us.

We are captivated by how he is dressed: "Now Joshua was standing before the angel, clothed with filthy garments" (verse 3). This was a mirror of his heart, a picture of his guilt and the guilt of the nation of Israel before God. Sometimes sin is described as a disease, other times it's simply called uncleanness. Here, Joshua is pictured as being dirty, guilty, and quite unable to do anything about it.

Joshua was much better than any common criminal. If we stood him alongside church members, he would still be more righteous than they. But that's not the standard of comparison: Joshua is in the presence of Someone more righteous than he; he is in the presence of "the angel of the Lord." If God were not so holy, our guilt would be manageable; but the divine standard is the Divine One Himself.

What do you think Joshua wanted to do at that moment? I'm sure he felt like running from the presence of the Lord. But he just stood there as a representative of the nation of Israel. He was declared guilty, bearing the shame of the nation. And he knew that in the presence of the angel of the Lord he was just as guilty as he felt he was!

I'm reminded of a young woman I counseled who'd just had a sexual fling a few days before. She not only knew her virginity was gone, but, she said, when the act was over, it was as if a voice said to

her, "Ha! Now you are dirty." The words she used to describe herself were the same as the word "filthy" used of Joshua's clothes. Yes,
filth. Excrement, to be exact.

The Lord Stands Beside Us

There was hope for Joshua, just as there is hope for those whose
consciences have driven them to despair. What was God saying?
What was the devil demanding?

Let's continue the story and take a closer look at this "angel of
the Lord." We have a clue as to who he is when we hear him say,
"The LORD rebuke you, O Satan! The LORD who has chosen Jerusalem rebuke you!" (verse 2). The angel of the Lord is called "LORD,"
and has the ability to forgive sins.

Most scholars agree that "*the* angel of the Lord" (as opposed to
an angel of the Lord) refers to Christ before He came to earth in
human flesh. Joshua was, in fact, standing in the presence of Jesus!

We stand condemned in the presence of holiness, the presence
of the One whose purity we must match. We stand exposed, spiritually naked.

But now we have some good news.

"The angel said to those who were standing before him, 'Remove
the filthy garments from him.' And to him he said, 'Behold, I have
taken your iniquity away from you, and I will clothe you with pure
vestments'" (verses 4-5). Evidently angels were on standby to do
the bidding of the angel of the Lord. So Joshua's filthy garments
were discarded.

Of course, he was not left naked. Clean clothes, "rich garments"
or "pure garments," were put on his shoulders. Now he could stand
before the angel of the Lord without shame.

Ponder something I've said before: The issue is not the greatness
of our sin but the beauty of the robes that cover us. We might ask,
"How filthy were Joshua's garments? Of what sins was he guilty?"

Interesting questions, but irrelevant because his filth was gone; his new garments were as clean as the ones worn by the angel of the Lord!

But there is more to be said.

Satan, the Accuser

We must understand Satan's role in this story.

In short, Satan gives this story a twist—he tries to change it from a scene of reconciliation to one of division. Rather than helping Joshua get reconciled to God, he tries to separate him from God. Joshua is standing before the angel, but "Satan [is] standing at his right hand to accuse him" (verse 1).

Think this through: Who's making these accusations? First, it's the one who is the embodiment of sin. If Joshua is dirty, Satan is dirtier yet. If Joshua is unclean, Satan is doubly so. No wonder demons who have the nature of their leader, Satan, are frequently called unclean spirits (see, for example, Matthew 12:43). They are completely dirty without a hint of goodness or a whiff of kindness. Nor can the world of evil spirits ever have their sins covered, because they're not included in God's plan to redeem humanity.

Second, the accusations are made by the one who is the instigator of sin. He tempted Adam and Eve to sin. Today, he continues to tempt us. He lures us into sin so that he can turn around and accuse us of being sinners! He's like a man who is both an arsonist and a firefighter: He constantly appears at disasters that he's helped create.

Third, Satan is motivated by hatred: hatred of God, and hatred of God's people. Blinded by rage, consumed with jealousy, and facing a humiliating future, he reminds us of our guilt and shame while we stand in the presence of God.

To us he says, "Just look at your dirty clothes! You say God has forgiven you. Really? Just remember what you did. You don't feel forgiven, do you? God is so mad at you...He'd prefer that you just go away."

Satan wants to convince us of our hopelessness; he wants us to turn away from God and commit more sins to deaden the pain that our past sins created. The evil one wants to separate us from fellowship with God; he wants to cut us off from the blessing of a clear conscience. He wants our sin to look bigger than God's grace.

Thankfully the angel of the Lord takes up our cause. He rebukes the devil's accusations. To be sure, we are great sinners, but God makes a huge distinction between what we deserve and the grace He will give us. Thanks to Jesus, God removes our sin and declares us to be as righteous as He Himself is. We're dressed in *God's* clothes.

Joshua was even given festal robes—that is, the clothes of a priest—so that he could function in the presence of God. Just so, we are priests before God and come into His presence with encouragement and confidence (see Hebrews 4:16).

The clean garments Joshua received represent the gift of righteousness given to us when we accept Christ as our sin-bearer. We are acquitted by God and declared to be as righteous as God Himself is. This qualifies us to be God's children.

Distinguishing the Voice of God from the Voice of Satan

What if Joshua had listened to the accusations of Satan and disregarded God's offer to receive clean clothes? What if Satan's loud voice had drowned out the voice of God? Thankfully, God gave a resounding *yes* to forgiveness even in the face of Satan's *no*.

Here are four instances in which we must be careful to distinguish the voice of God from the voice of Satan.

First, to the person who hears a voice that sometimes seems to say good things and at other times evil, I say: Realize that this voice is from Satan even when it may appear to have acceptable or even "biblical" messages. Satan can quote Scripture (see Matthew 4:5-6).

The good words are used by Satan to mask the evil. Satan, the master of deception, is willing to give you what you want to hear as long as you end up getting what he wants you to have.

Your first step is to receive the forgiveness and acceptance that God offers to all who trust Jesus as their Savior and Lord. These alien voices must be renounced; they must neither be believed nor allowed to distract. A book that would be helpful in this regard is *The Adversary*, by Mark Bubeck (published by Moody Publishers).

If a thief were to break into your house, that would not mean that the thief owns the house, only that he was trying to take what wasn't his. Just so, if you're a believer and you've placed your faith in Christ, Satan can never own you. He might harass you. He might play with your emotions and exploit the false guilt that's on your conscience. But realize that God would never ask you to do what you intuitively know is evil. You must listen to the voice of God in the Scriptures, not the restless voice of demonic spirits.

Second, if you are a believer and you've confessed your sins yet you still have a conscience that haunts you, remember that when you belong to God's family, the Holy Spirit convicts you of sin for which you must ask forgiveness, but once you have confessed that sin, His work is over. There is still, however, the matter of your relationship to other people who might need attention (which is addressed in a future chapter of this book). But as for your relationship with God, you can insist on a clear conscience.

In short, Satan accuses you of sins that have already been forgiven. He lies, not just with words, but with feelings. His hateful desire is to drive a wedge between you and God. Satan's trying to activate your conscience to make you think that you're beyond the reach of God's grace.

So, you can know Satan is accusing you whenever you feel the need to repeatedly confess your sins because you have no assurance of having been heard the first time. Of course, you must be sincere in your repentance and confession, but you do well to remember what John said in 1 John 1:9: "If we confess our sins, he is faithful and just to forgive us our sins and to cleanse us from all unrighteousness."

"What will I do with my unclean heart?" a woman asked me. "I can't take steel wool to my heart and scrub it." How right she was. Even the strongest extra-strength detergent can't get down to the nitty-gritty level of the conscience. There's no cure for deep regret, for alienation from God, or for self-loathing. Only God is able to reach down to the depth of our psyche and scrub it clean.

There are two gifts mentioned in 1 John 1:9. We are both forgiven and cleansed. Our fellowship with God is restored, and subjectively, our conscience is purged. There is a subjective cleansing that takes away your sin. This is your privilege as a Christian. Yes, you must accept God's forgiveness, but also His cleansing.

A woman who had been immoral in her youth still suffered from guilt and regret over her past sins. "I'm sure you've confessed your sins," I said.

"Oh yes, I have confessed those sins a thousand times," she replied.

I pointed out that we can't clear our consciences by confessing the same sins again and again. Indeed, the very act of reconfession is proof that we lack faith that God is "faithful and just to forgive, and to cleanse us." When nagging pangs of guilt return, we must affirm that our sins are already forgiven. Guilt serves a purpose in that it leads us to confess our sins to God; but once we have accepted His forgiveness, guilt serves no useful purpose. God says you're forgiven, and from His point of view, it's a done deal. Nevertheless, Satan wants us to think that we still haven't suffered enough.

Charles Spurgeon illustrated, in a moving sermon, the lengths God will go to in covering our sins:

Man piles a mountain of sin, but God will match it, and
he raises up a loftier mountain of grace; man heaps up a
still larger hill of sin, but the Lord surpasses it with ten
times more grace; and so the contest continues until at
last the mighty God pulls up the mountains by the roots
and buries man's sin beneath them as a fly might be buried beneath an Alp. Abundant sin is no barrier to the
superabundant grace of God.[1]

Abundant sin is no barrier to the superabundant grace of God!

Third, Satan is involved when you think that you must suffer for
your sin. You may think that if you berate yourself enough times,
if you live under a cloud of constant condemnation (which admittedly all of us deserve), you are thereby making true forgiveness
more likely. But no. You do not have to berate yourself or inflict
pain on your body. Forgiveness is a free gift to those who receive
it. Once again you're faced with either believing God or believing
your emotions, which frequently deceive you.

Fourth, you can be certain Satan is involved when a person has
been forgiven by God but people whom he's offended in the past
insist that he's not really repentant. Of course it's possible that the
person isn't truly repentant, but here's a scenario I've observed several times.

I've seen this most clearly in instances where a man has committed adultery, has repented, and has asked his wife for forgiveness. He himself is devastated, incredulous that he could ever be
unfaithful to the woman he married and loves. He repents openly
before his wife and others. His wife is devastated, but over time she
says she chooses to forgive him and stay committed to their marriage. But she, out of understandable anger and betrayal, won't let
him forget what he did to her. She keeps telling him that his confession was insincere; she thinks honesty demands that they con-
tinually readdress his failure.

Is she right or wrong? Does honesty require that this sin be referred to repeatedly in their arguments? And does it have to be mentioned in the future if he wishes to be involved in some level of Christian ministry? Or is this Satan's way of making sure that they can make no progress in their relationship and that they must always speak and act as if the sin had just occurred? In short, their past is never allowed to rest.

The attitude and work of the devil affects usually everyone involved both in needing and accepting forgiveness. Sometimes the person who is asked to forgive the penitent has a greater need than the person who requested the forgiveness. Trust is very fragile and takes time to rebuild, but a sincere expression of repentance should be accepted.

Talk is cheap. To say that you have forgiven is not the same as burying the hatchet. As someone said, "We buried the hatchet, but a path led to its shallow grave."

Responding to Satan

When we see Satan thrown out of heaven by Michael, the archangel, we read, "The accuser of our brothers has been thrown down, who accuses them day and night before our God. And they have conquered him by the blood of the Lamb and by the word of their testimony, for they loved not their lives even unto death" (Revelation 12:10-11).

Here is Satan accusing people whom God has acquitted. They conquered Satan's attacks by affirming the value and victory of "the blood of the Lamb." Just so, we must stand on the ground of Scripture and not listen to the accusations about sins that God has declared forgiven.

We must counter Satan's accusations with, "Who shall bring any charge against God's elect? It is God who justifies. Who is to condemn? Christ Jesus is the one who died—more than that, who was raised—who is at the right hand of God, who indeed is inter-ceding for us" (Romans 8:33-34).

We can confidently say, "The Lord rebuke you, Satan!"

The prophet Isaiah wrote, "In love you have delivered my life from the pit of destruction, for you have cast all my sins behind your back" (Isaiah 38:17). Imagine two roads: one is clean and well-traveled; the other is wretched, with deep ruts that veer off into a ditch. When a heavy snowfall blankets the two roads, both are equally covered. Just so, our sins, big and small, are equally covered by God: "Though your sins are like scarlet, they shall be as white as snow; though they are red like crimson, they shall become like wool" (Isaiah 1:18). Your sins might still be on your mind, but they are not on His! He says, "I have blotted out your transgressions like a cloud and your sins like mist" (Isaiah 44:2).

Joshua reminds us that our guilt should drive us toward God, not away from Him. Our natural instinct to run should be repressed; we must come into God's presence without excuses and pretense. *Guilt is not God trying to push us away from Him, but rather God trying to put His arms around us.*

God Honors All Whom He Forgives

Joshua did not merely have new garments, but a clean turban. He was restored to priestly ministry and was given a special assignment. I recently heard the testimony of a former heroin addict who served time in prison for armed robbery. After he became a believer and accepted God's forgiveness for his many sins, he was hired as a supervisor in a Christian organization. He said, "The fact that I—a scumbag—was told that I could be used of God drove me to my knees in thankfulness to God."

The movie *The Shawshank Redemption* is a story of prison life in the Northeast in the late 1940s and early 1950s. The film focuses on the journey of two men's hearts through the trials and temptations of prison life. Red, the ringleader and most seasoned of the prisoners, explains what happens when you live within those walls too long. He says that "at first you hate the walls, and then they drive you crazy. But eventually you adapt to them and aren't aware of them anymore. Then you come to realize you need them."

We could paraphrase a sinner's story in much the same way: You begin by hating your dirty clothes of anger, addictions, and deception, but then you get used to them. And then you prefer them. And eventually you need them. That's the most tragic day of all—the day when you prefer slavery to freedom; you prefer your dirty clothes to the clean ones God has waiting for you.

In his classic allegory *The Pilgrim's Progress*, John Bunyan likened sin to a burden on the conscience that can be removed only by God. We aren't doing God any favors when we try to manage our sin on our own. Instead, we honor Him when we admit that we need not only His help, but His intervention.

In the end, forgiven sin has only as much power as we let it have. Or as much power as we let Satan have with it. Yes, the memories of our sin might come to mind. We may experience some of the old guilt and self-condemnation. But we must respond by affirming, "God has spoken on the matter, and I believe His Word."

Satan's primary weapon against us is guilt; our primary weapon against him is the assurance of our complete forgiveness.

A Passage to Ponder:

God made [us] alive together with him, having forgiven us all of our trespasses, by canceling the record of debt that stood against us with its legal demands. This he set aside, nailing it to his cross. *He disarmed the rulers and authorities and put them to open shame, by triumphing over them in him*" (Colossians 2:13-15, emphasis added).

Probing Questions to Consider:

Can you think of an instance in your own life in which Satan won a victory? What could you have done to resist him? How can you prepare for his assaults against your mind and emotions?

Ask God for wisdom as to how to discern between Satan's work and the promptings of the Holy Spirit.

No Condemnation:
No Need for Suicide

By saying that we cannot forgive ourselves,
we elevate our judgment above the Lord's.
We think that we know better than He does;
He *might be quick to forgive, but we are not so simple.*
Yet what right do we have to hang onto
something that God released?[1]

CHARLES SWINDOLL

Fox Lake Lt. Joseph Gliniewicz didn't have to commit suicide. Back in 2015, he staged an elaborate suicide hoax, pretending to have been killed by three men who were approaching him. After an extensive search, the men were never found, and further investigation proved that he had actually committed suicide. Damaging information about him was about to be exposed, and he couldn't face his tarnished future that might have also landed him in jail. Better to die at his own hand, he thought, than to face the shame that awaited him.

Lady Macbeth gave us a vivid description of the agony of conscience, the torment of a person who tries to manage guilt on her own. She had participated in the murder of King Duncan.

> Out, damned spot! out I say!...What need we fear who knows it, when none can call our power to account?

[She is saying, "We are in such a position of privilege nobody is going to get even with us. Why should we fear?"] Yet who would have thought the old man to have had so much blood in him...Will these hands ne'er be clean?...Here's the smell of the blood still. All the perfumes of Arabia will not sweeten this little hand...Oh, what a sigh is there! The heart is sorely charged...All the oceans of the world would not wash the blood from my hand. Rather, my hands would make the seas red.[2]

Reread those words and notice her attempt to suppress guilt. She assured herself that she was too powerful to be prosecuted; she washed her hands fervently, symbolically trying to scrub her heart. And she hoped against hope that perfume would sweeten the stench of her foul hands.

But the more she obsessed over her condemning conscience, the greater her crime appeared. If she could wash it away, the ocean would become bloody, but her hands would still have the smell of blood.

Tragically, Lady Macbeth, with no relief from her plagued conscience, did what 35,000 Americans do every year—she committed suicide. Her guilt simply couldn't be wished away.

In Chicago, where I live, I'm aware of several teenagers—*Christian* teenagers—who committed suicide. One of them left a note that said, "I've messed up too many times."

Sad. And unnecessary.

The purpose of this chapter is to help those who are so overwhelmed by their guilt that they're driven to despair. Certainly not all depression and mental illness is because of guilt, but much of it can be traced to a conscience that simply doesn't give them rest.

Our feelings often tell us lies. Our emotions can tell us lies about ourselves, lies about our value as a person, and lies about our hopelessness as we face the future. Thankfully, these lies don't have to be believed. These condemning voices are silenced when we accept the promises of God.

A chaplain asked a drug addict, "Why do you take drugs?"

He replied, "Chaplain, you ought to know the answer to that question without me telling you. Sure, I know. I feel so bad about some of the things I've done, I want to die. I don't have the guts to pick up a gun and blow my brains out, so I just do it the slow way with drugs. I feel like I ought to pay for what all I've done wrong. I think that most of us who use this stuff feel the same way."[3]

Because the past can't be changed, it's easy to believe that the future is fixed. We see only despair, regret, and emptiness. We see only sleepless nights, the condemnation of others, and unbearable shame. And hopelessness.

This chapter is dedicated to this premise: No matter how heavily your conscience may weigh upon you, no matter the regret and the despair, there is hope. There is hope in God. You can be brought into His presence honored, welcomed, worthy, and completely forgiven. No matter who you are, there is still a place for you in God's world.

Stay with me.

Read these verses from the book of Hebrews:

> If the blood of goats and bulls, and the sprinkling of defiled persons with the ashes of a heifer, sanctify for the purification of the flesh, *how much more will the blood of Christ, who through the eternal Spirit offered himself without blemish to God, purify our conscience from dead works to serve the living God* (Hebrews 9:13-17, emphasis added).

> ...let us draw near with a true heart in full assurance of faith, *with our hearts sprinkled clean from an evil conscience* and our bodies washed with pure water (10:22).

Two similar phrases should catch our attention. The first one is "purify our conscience," and the second is "sprinkled clean from an evil conscience." Peace is available for you despite your past.

The Power of Blood Atonement

In order to understand why the author of Hebrews puts so much value on the blood of Christ and its ability to cleanse us, we need a bit of Old Testament background.

God was about to judge Egypt for its pagan rebellion as seen in its worship of various gods. In the last of ten plagues, God said He would destroy the firstborn son in every home in Egypt, but the Israelites would be exempt if they followed specific directions.

On the day before the judgment, God asked the Israelites to take a lamb, one that was as perfect as they could find, and put its blood on the doorposts of their houses. "Then they shall take some of the blood and put it on the two doorposts and the lintel of the houses in which they eat it" (Exodus 12:7). And here was the promise:

> I will pass through the land of Egypt that night, and I will strike all the firstborn in the land of Egypt...The blood shall be a sign for you, on the houses where you are. And when I see the blood, I will pass over you (verses 12-13).

That's why it's called the *Passover*. The angel of death would not enter a house that had the blood on the door. The blood proved that an animal had been killed as a substitute for the oldest son in the house. So to paraphrase, God said, "When I see the blood, I'll pass over you because I'll see that an animal died in the place of the firstborn, and so you won't come under judgment."

Imagine a Jewish family with a firstborn son, a teenager, who struggled with depression. He was a burden to his parents and refused to cooperate with his siblings. As long as there was blood on their door, the angel of death would not enter. It wasn't the good disposition of the family that mattered; it was blood that mattered.

Let's go a step further and suppose that that teenager was a very bad child, far worse than some of the Egyptian firstborns. I would feel sorry for his parents if that were the case, but as far as the judgment was concerned, their home was protected. God was saying, in effect, "I'm not looking at the conduct of this household, I'm looking for the blood."

In other words, the blood was independent of how the family was living; it was unaffected by their piety or lack of it. Whether it was a happy household or filled with conflict, illness, or depression, it mattered not. Blood was their protection.

The Precious Blood of Christ

And yet the blood of lambs was only symbolic of the blood of Jesus that would actually remove our sins. One day, John the Baptist pointed to Jesus and announced, "Behold, the Lamb of God, who takes away the sin of the world!" (John 1:29). Later in the New Testament we read that the blood of Jesus Christ is precious, something not said about the blood of lambs. The blood of Jesus alone was able to serve as our substitute in taking our guilt and making us right with God.

Stay with me on this.

So in Hebrews 9:12-14 we are told that, in contrast to the sacrifices of the Old Testament, the blood of Jesus would now *"purify our conscience from dead works to serve the living God"* (emphasis added).

What does it mean to be purified "from dead works? What is a dead work? In short, it's religious rituals performed time and time again that never bring the cleansing and assurance of forgiveness. They're called "dead works" because they have no means by which to cleanse our conscience. Dead works are powerless; they're unable to resolve our guilt and set us free.

Deliverance from Dead Works

The greatest mistake people make is to try to clear their conscience with dead works. They insist that they have to play a part in the cleansing by some means of self-salvation. Yes, indeed, God will help them, but they believe they have to have a part to help "even the score." No wonder they never move beyond a focus on their past.

So what are some of these dead works?

Old Testament sacrifices are dead works. The sacrifices were commanded in the Old Testament, but with the coming of Christ, they must no longer be offered. Some of the people to whom the book of Hebrews was written said to themselves, "We don't know about this Jesus and the teaching that His sacrifice on the cross accomplished our redemption once for all; we had better return to animal sacrifices." But sacrifices were dead works that could never cleanse their conscience.

The Mass is a dead work. In the mass, Jesus is offered again and again, and somehow His work is never seen as totally, completely finished. Indeed, the book of Hebrews speaks of those who "are crucifying once again the Son of God to their own harm" (Hebrews 6:6). Even if the mass could take away past sins (which it can't), there's no guarantee of forgiveness for the future. Those who participate might feel better for a time, but they have no assurance of permanent forgiveness.

Baptism can be a dead work. I've baptized many people upon their profession of faith in Christ. But baptism is a step of obedience for a believer, not a means of salvation. Sadly, there are millions of people who are trusting in their baptism (usually infant baptism) to make them Christians and to give them special access to God. But alas, there is no assurance that their relationship with God is settled forever.

Confession can be a dead work. Martin Luther confessed his sins daily and thoroughly but never found peace for his conscience. His confessor, Johann von Staupitz, grew so weary of Luther's confessions that he said, in essence, "The next time come with some big sins, not all these little peccadilloes. Let it be murder, or something like that."

But Luther was a better theologian than some of his contemporaries. He knew that the question was not whether a sin was big or little but whether it had been confessed. His problem was that even if he could remember all of his sins and confess them, the next day would bring new sins that had to be identified and confessed. Confession gave him temporary relief until his mind became aware of some possible new sins he had committed. Confession would not silence his conscience.

Good works can be dead works. There are people today who do charitable deeds because it makes them feel better; they think that surely God is going to look down and weigh their good works against their bad works and hopefully the scales will be tipped in their favor.

I have a friend who said that whenever he came home and mowed the lawn without being asked, his mother would say to him, "Well, what have you been up to now?" In other words, "For what misdeed are you making atonement?" Some people use good works to even the score and make up for their sins. But works can't even the score.

Physical punishment is a dead work. In some cultures, self-atonement is taken to the extreme. On television I've seen people flagellate themselves, whip themselves, and even allow individuals to temporarily crucify themselves in the hope that God will say, "Your sacrifice is truly painful and I'm impressed with the lengths to which you are going to make atonement. Thus I will receive you."

But all forms of self-salvation bring only uncertainty and the inner desire for more punishment. Teenagers (adults too) slash their wrists not because they want to kill themselves (though some do), but because they feel so devalued by their parents or peers or others. Many feel guilty for just being alive. They tell themselves, "I can't just receive God's grace freely. Rather, I need to suffer, I expect to suffer, and I deserve to suffer because God would never accept me."

Others say, "Lord, You really ought to receive me today because I had a warm devotional time." Or, "Lord, you ought to receive me because I'm not as bad as other people. Do you know what so-and-so did, Lord? I'm better than that, and you know that I'm trying hard to be good. I promise." None of that helps.

We must reject any attempt at self-atonement. I believe the greatest mistake many people make when coming before God in prayer is to look at their lives and try to find some reason God should accept them. But they never find the right formula for their anxious souls.

But there is good news for all of us.

A Once-for-All Sacrifice

We have to step off the "good works" treadmill if we want to find permanent peace with God. For that we look to Jesus, who made a once-for-all sacrifice that brings about cleansing from any evil conscience.

To see the superiority of Jesus over the Old Testament sacrifices, read these words:

> Every priest stands daily at his service, offering repeatedly the same sacrifices, which can never take away sins. But when Christ had offered *for all time a single sacrifice for sins*, he sat down at the right hand of God, waiting

from that time until his enemies should be made a footstool for his feet. For by a *single* offering he has perfected *for all time* those who are being sanctified" (Hebrews 10:11-14, emphasis added).

We can't miss the point. Thanks to Jesus, the work is totally finished. The author of Hebrews makes four contrasts between the priests of the Old Testament and Jesus, our High Priest.

The Old Testament era is gone and the New has come.

1. Rather than many priests (who worked in eight hour shifts), Jesus is now the one and only Priest.

2. Rather than many sacrifices, Jesus offered Himself, the One and only Sacrifice.

3. Rather than standing as the priests did (indicating that their work was never done), Jesus sat down because His work was completely finished.

4. Rather than the worshipper bringing an offering, Jesus Himself is the offering that can "perfect us forever."

This is what Martin Luther needed to understand. He needed to know there was a work of God which was so sufficient that he could have the assurance that he belonged to God forever. Once he discovered this, Luther didn't have to wonder if he was missing a sin during confession. By accepting Christ's sacrifice through faith in Christ, Luther was permanently reborn. Only the sacrifice of Christ, the shedding of His blood, could do what "dead works" can't.

Full Access to God

And there is more.

Let's keep reading. Because of Jesus' sacrifice, we're given this promise: "we have confidence to enter the holy places by the blood of Jesus" (10:19). Access is all-important because it is in the presence of God that sins are forgiven.

In the temple there were two sacred areas. One was called the holy place, where all priests could enter. It contained three items: the altar of incense, the table of showbread, and the candlestick. But only the high priest could enter the inner sanctuary called the Holy of Holies, the very dwelling place of God, to offer the blood of atonement for the people's sins.

So in the Old Testament, entering God's presence was limited to one person on one day a year. But Hebrews 10:19 says the blood of Jesus has given us "confidence ['boldness,' KJV] to enter into the holy places." That includes both the holy place and the inner sanctuary, where God dwelt.

Please understand this: When we come to God on the basis of the blood of Christ, He says, in effect, "If you come because your faith is in the blood of Jesus, you are welcome in My very presence. Your sins are no longer a barrier between us."

There's even more imagery we should be aware of from the Jewish temple at Jerusalem. A thick curtain hung between the holy place and the Holy of Holies. When Jesus dismissed His spirit and died on the cross, the Bible tells us what happened: "And behold, the curtain of the temple was torn in two, from top to bottom" (Matthew 27:51). It was torn from the top down because God did it. And it was torn to show that we now have access to God, through Christ.

As Jesus' side was pierced with a sword, and his body ripped from the cross, just so, the curtain that separated common people from the Holy of Holies had been ripped in two. Thanks to Jesus and His blood that was shed on the cross, we can come into the very presence of Almighty God.

We don't come to God saying, "Well, I wonder if I've done

enough. I wonder if You are going to accept what I've done. Am I good enough? Look at my past. Look at my background."

"Since we have a great priest over the house of God, let us draw near with a true heart in full assurance of faith" (Hebrews 10:21-22). We come to God because He says, "I so value the blood of Christ that if you come through Him, come boldly. You will be gladly received."

What does it mean to come to God "with our hearts sprinkled clean from an evil conscience"? When the Old Testament priest was carrying out the prescribed rituals in the temple, he sprinkled blood on all of the articles within as a symbol of their being cleansed. So the writer was saying, "In the very same way, symbolically, the blood of Jesus Christ is applied to our consciences."

Obviously, our consciences are not literally sprinkled with blood, but Christ's blood is so effective that we can experience freedom and deliverance from an evil conscience. And the conclusion? "Let us hold fast the confession of our hope without wavering, for he who promised is faithful" (verse 23).

Keep reading.

The Path to a Clear Conscience

Depression, hopelessness, regret, and overwhelming guilt. The blood of Christ gives us acceptance before God independent of our performance. As with the Israelites in Egypt, God sees the blood of His Son and our sins are wiped out; we stand without condemnation.

You may be struggling with same-sex attraction; you may have entered into an immoral relationship. You may say, "I'm different. I don't fit in." But the good news is that you belong with the rest of us at the cross of Christ. You can come to God freely and unhindered if you're coming to Him trusting in the blood of Christ to get you there.

There was a famous evangelist—both a Bible teacher and a scholar—who was dying with fear and distress. This man's friends said to him, "Think of all you have done; you were the president of a school, you wrote books, you were an effective pastor." But this brought no peace. And then somebody reminded him of what he already knew: "The only basis upon which we receive entry into God's presence is through the blood of Christ, and it is enough." This great man died in peace. Remember that the blood of Christ is the only basis upon which we come to God.

Don't get confused on this point. We can enjoy the freedom of a clear conscience despite the ongoing consequences of our sin. A young woman can be completely forgiven for her immorality, but she must deal with her pregnancy and the birth of a child.

Yes, King David killed Uriah, the husband of Bathsheba, the woman with whom he had an affair. He tried to cover up his sinful deeds, but it didn't go well. When confronted, he admitted to his wrongdoing, which restored his joy in God. But the consequences of what he had done continued on in the lives of his dysfunctional children.

When David confessed his sin, he asked for a clear conscience and said, "Wash me, and I shall be whiter than snow (Psalm 51:7). If you melt snow in a bucket, after it melts, there will be a small amount of residue at the bottom because snow is not completely pure. That's why David asked God to wash him "whiter" than snow.

Then David prayed, "Let me hear joy and gladness; let the bones that you have broken rejoice...Restore to me the joy of your salvation" (verses 8,12). He would not allow his sin to define who he was; he accepted God's joy despite the mess he'd created.

We might say to David, "Come on! You're asking God to restore your joy? You wrecked your family. You lost all moral authority over your sons, four of whom died because of your sin. There's no way you can restore Bathsheba's purity. Uriah, the man you killed, can't be raised from the dead. And yet you want to rejoice in God again?"

David would probably answer this way: "I left a terrible mess, but God's forgiveness is so great that I can still rejoice in the God of my salvation. The consequences do not stop me from saying that God accepts me. My conscience has stopped condemning me."

It's Not Feelings, But Faith

Would an airline bar you from getting on a plane because you felt unworthy, or if you had a migraine, or had just sinned against your conscience? All an airline cares about is whether you have a ticket. Your being allowed on board is independent of what is going on in your life. "Just show me your ticket, please."

Neither Lady Macbeth or Sergeant Gliniewicz had to commit suicide. If they had known what Jesus had done on behalf of sinners and embraced this for themselves, they could have cleared their consciences before God. Of course they would still have had to face the consequences of their crimes. But when the conscience has been cleansed by God, a person can face the ridicule of others and the shame of exposure.

Of course it isn't easy. If Gliniewicz, for example, had been honest in his confession before his peers and the media, he would still have had to go to jail. But he could have lived with himself in fellowship with God. As for the teenager who said, "I've messed up too many times," the answer is "No, you have not." There is no limit to God's forgiveness for those who come in repentance and faith.

The bottom line is that we must have such firm trust in what Jesus has done for us that we choose to disbelieve our feelings of worthlessness, residual guilt, and hopelessness. Depression and regret don't reflect reality. Feelings say, "There's no hope! You are

so bad the world would be better off if you were to end your life."
That is a lie! Even Judas would not have been driven to suicide if he
had repented in the presence of the one he betrayed.

When the time comes that this world will be better off without you, God will call for you and take you home. He knows your
name and your address. Let Him make that decision. What you
need to do is confront these lies and retrain your conscience. A
defiled conscience produces unbelief, anxiety, fear, and hopelessness. A cleansed conscience produces assurance, peace, and hope.

Thankfully, no sin is unpardonable. In the dozens of promises
in the New Testament regarding salvation, the invitation is never
restricted because somebody committed a sin that was too big. For
God, the issue is never the greatness of the sin, but the willingness
of the sinner to believe the good news of the gospel.

This is a lesson I've learned throughout the years. In my dis-
couragement, in times when I think, *I really blew it there*, I always
have to remember to say, "God, I'm so thankful that the basis of
my acceptance is Your Son's blood, and I accept that blood as my
cleansing and my forgiveness."

I want to borrow some words from the great civil rights leader
Dr. Martin Luther King, Jr., using them in a different context. If
you understand the truths we have considered in this chapter, you
can say, "Free at last! Free at last! Thank God Almighty, I'm free
at last!"

We can endure almost anything if our conscience has been
cleansed by God. A clear conscience enables us to sleep well and
live even better.

A Passage to Ponder:

Therefore, brothers, since we have confidence to enter the holy places by the blood of Jesus, by the new and living way that he opened for us through the curtain, that is, through his flesh, and since we have a great priest over the house of God, let us draw near with a true heart in full assurance of faith, with our hearts sprinkled clean from an evil conscience (Hebrews 10:19-22).

Probing Questions to Consider:

This time, rather than answer questions, let us pray the passage we have been studying together:

O Lord Jesus, thank You for dying and rising from the dead to secure my salvation. I receive the benefits of the work Your blood accomplished. I give You my past, which I cannot change; I give You the sins I have committed, and also those sins committed against me.

I enter into Your presence with the steady assurance that I am gladly welcomed and received. I stand against the accusations of my conscience and the restlessness of my inner spirit. I thank You that Your work is complete, once-for-all, and entirely sufficient for my need. I thank You for hearing me and receiving me.

I pray this prayer to the Father, the Son, and the Spirit. Your promises will always be my joy and hope.

In Jesus' name. Amen.

5

The Truth That Hurts and Heals

There is only one way to achieve happiness
on this terrestrial ball, and that is to have
either a clear conscience, or none at all.

OGDEN NASH, AMERICAN HUMORIST

There is a story about a cocaine addict in New York who decided to chain himself to a radiator in his room so that he wouldn't go down on the street to get more cocaine. But apparently he was able to break a piece of metal from the radiator to which he had chained himself, and he carried it with him onto the street so that he could get another fix. He explained his bizarre actions by saying, "Coke has a voice, and when it calls, I must go."

Cocaine is not the only addiction that has a voice. So do alcoholism, gambling, pornography, and various sexual addictions. It's difficult to have a conscience that's free when there's always a shadow within our hearts, a reminder that we are living with unconquered sin and repeated failure.

I am under no illusions that simply reading this chapter will free a person from an addiction; almost certainly the stronghold is too powerful for that. What I do intend is to point the way to victory in the battle. The path is hard, but it's worthwhile.

Characteristics of Addictions

Many excellent books have been written on overcoming addictions, but I offer these five observations with the prayer that they will shed some light on this vicious cycle and point the way out of the darkness.

First, I want to emphasize the need for grace. Addicts don't need more guilt heaped on them; they already bear the weight of condemnation. Their defiled conscience reminds them that they have no ladder with which to climb out of a dark hole. They need to read chapter 4 of this book, which emphasizes that God accepts them on the basis of Christ's blood rather than their flawed attempts to be good.

Addicts must be assured that God is on their side in their struggles. Yes, they'll also need friends to help them, but God is available for their fellowship, their acceptance, and their worship. God shines a shaft of light into their dark world. We must begin with grace.

Second, we are all prone to be addicts. We all love something more than we should. The prophet Ezekiel spoke about the people of Israel who had "taken their idols into their hearts, and set the stumbling block of their iniquity before their faces" (Ezekiel 14:3). Some addictions are obvious and known, others are more subtle or secret. So rather than identifying who is an addict and who isn't, it's time that we think of addiction in terms of a continuum, knowing that all of us struggle with sin at some level. We're all on a journey and not a one of us has arrived. Even when we have been brought to the light, we are prone to retreat back into the darkness.

Almost every family in the United States has been affected by addiction. So let's not deceive ourselves; instead, let's humbly admit that the default position of our sinful nature is toward addiction. Admitting our need is the first step toward wholeness.

Third, grace does not enter closed doors. This is critical to understand. Even as you read this statement, you may already be thinking of reasons why you are the way you are, and why you can't afford to change. If this is your attitude, I assure you that God's grace is open and inviting. God doesn't have His back toward you—He's facing you with His arms wide open.

At one time I was naive enough to believe that if I just told people what they should do, they could walk away from their addictions. The formula was pretty simple: Memorize verses from the Bible, learn certain principles, pray, and yield to God. Go home and apply these principles, and you'll be free! But the more years I've lived, the more I've come to realize that sinful patterns of behavior are deeply entrenched. The rationalizations of the human heart go down to bedrock. Excuses abound. Blindness exists in all of us. We must all turn away from our desire to hide. We need to come to God and invite trusted friends into our lives, bringing our sin with us.

Fourth, addictions have many causes. If you were brought up in an addictive home, living with alcoholism, drugs, or immorality, it's possible that you grew up with an addictive personality. So even if you conquer one addiction, you might simply substitute it for another. Or perhaps a friend at school or at work might have introduced you to drugs or alcohol or pornography. You may have discovered that an addiction makes life a lot better until it makes life a lot worse—much worse.

Whatever the cause, the real problem is our hearts. Someone has well said that *an addiction is an illusory promise creating a world of escape.* The addict enters into a world of pleasurable sensations: It promises like a god, but in the end, pays like a devil.

Fifth, there are many, many different "matches" that set fire to addictions. The instant access to pornography on the internet has made us all vulnerable in a way that wasn't possible twenty years ago. And of course there are other addictions you can feed online—you can play occult video games, gamble, and hook up with a partner. The different ways to enter the cycle of repetitive sin are endless.

And so the secret life of an addict grows. He lives for his euphoria, this trance when he can be alone enjoying his favorite pastime. His inner life might be rotting, but it's hidden beneath an outer mask of normalcy and trumped-up happiness. Eventually when the inner life takes over, the outer life falls apart.

We're all prone to self-deception; we long to be deceived. Another definition of addiction is "the blinding absorption of sin." An addict can't see how his sin affects others; it blinds him to the devastation of what he's doing to himself and his future. When addicts have flashes of insight as to the horrible path they are on, these thoughts are quickly dismissed, ignored, and barred from entry into the mind. And so, in the midst of a hard life, the addiction brings them to a place of euphoria where nothing else matters except the fulfillment of their desires. They, in effect, say, "I'll take the devil's hand and deal with the consequences later."

Information is helpful, but we need someone to pull us out of the pit. Jesus must enter our world.

Set Free by the Son

Jesus had much to say about the power of sin and the path to freedom. On one occasion, as He spoke to a crowd, this exchange took place:

> "If you abide in my word, you are truly my disciples, and you will know the truth, and the truth will set you free." They answered him, "We are offspring of Abraham and have never been enslaved to anyone. How is it that you say, 'You will become free?'" Jesus answered them, "Truly, truly, I say to you, everyone who practices sin is a slave to sin. The slave does not remain in the house

forever; the son remains forever. So if the Son sets you free, you will be free indeed" (John 8:31-36).

Let's unpack these words.

Jesus was addressing two groups that day. Hearing Him were true believers (His disciples, for example), and these are the ones He exhorted to continue in His word and thereby become His disciples. These disciples would know the truth that would set them free.

But there was also a larger, unbelieving crowd of Jewish people who were offended by Jesus' words and so defended themselves: "We are offspring of Abraham and have never been enslaved to anyone." You can almost hear them spitting these words out of their mouth, making sure that Jesus got the point. To paraphrase, they were so offended by Jesus that they, in effect, asked, "Who do you think you're talking to? What do we need to be set free *from*?"

Slavery was common in Jesus' day. Everyone knew a slave could be bought, sold, or traded. A slave could be here today and gone tomorrow. In that context, Jesus said, "Everyone who practices sin is a slave to sin. The slave does not remain in the house forever; the son remains forever." What a powerful illustration of sin. But, Jesus added, "So if the Son sets you free, you will be free indeed."

This Way to Freedom

Here are three truths that point the way to deliverance from unconquered sin.

Know Thyself

We have to know our own hearts and admit that we take delight in being self-deceived. The self-righteous Pharisees declared (and you can hear the pride in their voices) that they had never been slaves to sin. "We're the righteous ones. We go to the temple. We pray. We keep the law. What more could you ask?" Their self-righteousness closed them off to the possibility of experiencing God's grace. They refused to repent of their self-righteousness.

We dare not underestimate our blindness to our own spiritual need. Morally, we are weaker than we think. Or to put it differently, we must not overestimate our ability to stop the cycle of failure by self-will or by learning some new technique, some new idea. In a book entitled *The Last Addiction*, the author, who herself had been an alcoholic, writes: "This great, unspeakable gift of addiction has been to teach me that *I cannot set myself free. I must be set free*"[1] (emphasis from the author).

Don't hurry over this. The point she is making is that the very last addiction is the belief that we can get out of our predicament alone—simply by sheer willpower, by memorizing verses, by promising ourselves that we won't do it again, or by making adjustments to our behavior. The idea that the self that got us into trouble is the self that can get us out of trouble is an illusion.

Recently I took a stress test. The doctor put me on a treadmill and said, "At first, you'll be able to keep up with the treadmill. But eventually you'll lose; the treadmill will win." For the first three minutes I thought, *Hey, this isn't bad at all. Just a fast walk.* But after three minutes he increased the incline, then the speed, and yes, I have to admit that the treadmill won. And it always will.

Catch this: The root meaning of the word *addiction* is "to surrender to the gods." At the end of the day, we surrender to false gods. It's a myth that we can rid ourselves of the power of these gods. Sin is deeper, and the devil is stronger. Self-rescuing from addiction is a fantasy we want to believe, but a fantasy it is. It is the *last* addiction.

Knowing the Schemes of Satan

In Jesus' interchange with the Jews, things quickly became heated. Jesus was very gentle, except when He was dealing with self-righteous people. They had claimed Abraham as their father, so Jesus gave them some strong words: "I know that you are offspring of Abraham; yet you seek to kill me because my word finds no place in you. I speak of what I have seen with my Father, and you do what you have heard from your father" (verses 37-38).

They responded by saying that Abraham was their father. Jesus disagreed: "You are of your father the devil, and your will is to do your father's desires. He was a murderer from the beginning [the devil is never interested in life, always death] and does not stand in the truth, because there is no truth in him. When he lies, he speaks out of his own character, for he is a liar and the father of lies" (verse 44).

Don't use that kind of language when telling your friends about Jesus! Jesus needed to jerk these braggarts into reality. He used much gentler language with those who were great sinners and knew it. The reaction of these self-righteous religious types, was to reject the truth about themselves, and then pick up stones to kill Jesus (verse 59). The bottom line is that they were believing the devil's lies rather than Jesus' truth.

The devil has two different sets of lies. To the Jews who were resisting Jesus, his lie was, "You're righteous. You go to the temple. You're not a drunkard. You're not with prostitutes. You pay your tithe, and you're very meticulous in keeping the law. You're okay as long as you belong to this club." But it was a lie. They were not okay before God.

There was only one way for these deluded, self-righteous people to see their own sin and trust Jesus to save them, and that was for God to overcome their self-chosen blindness and show them the real state of their hearts. Truth be told, God must do that for each one of us because we're so prone to self-deception. That's why Jesus said that the prostitutes and tax collectors go into the kingdom of heaven ahead of the self-righteous Pharisees (see Matthew 21:31-32).

There is another lie that Satan pawns off on us. It's tailor-made for those seeking a way out of their addiction: "You'll never change, and furthermore, you're worthless. You are unloved. You don't have any real value as a person. Look at your past. Look at what people think of you. Are you accepted? *No!* Are you a failure? *Yes.* You have every right to hate yourself, considering who you are. You have every right to slash your wrists in anger. You have every right to be anorexic so that you can angrily prove that you can control everything in your life."

Those kinds of thoughts come from Satan, and we must resist him and his words. We resist him through the Word of God (as Jesus did in the desert), and prayer, through fellowship with other believers, and through healthy relationships and accountability. Jesus said the devil is the original and the biggest liar. We have to identify his lies and disbelieve them.

Knowing God

Besides knowing something about ourselves and something about Satan, we need to know something about God. He is gracious and merciful. He gives us the gift of His presence, going with us into the darkest closets of our lives. He invites us to open the doors and let light shine in to deal with hidden patterns that have plagued us for years. So we turn to His path for us along the way.

Toward Freedom

Here are some pointers to ponder on your journey to freedom.

We Cannot Set Ourselves Free

I've already stressed it: We can't set ourselves free; we must be set free. Remember the words of Jesus: "You will know the truth, and the truth will set you free" (John 8:32). And even more importantly, we read, "So if the Son sets you free, you will be free indeed" (verse 36). Jesus has to enter our world if we are to be set free.

Centuries earlier, David wrote, "I waited patiently for the LORD; he inclined to me and heard my cry. He drew me up from the pit of destruction, out of the miry bog, and set my feet upon a rock, making my steps secure. He put a new song in my mouth, a song of praise to our God. Many will see and fear, and put their trust in the LORD" (Psalm 40:1-3).

When David was in the pit, God didn't say to Him, "Now David, here's a shovel. Dig yourself out." Why? If you try to dig yourself out of a pit, you're only going to dig yourself in deeper. Even if you have the determination to say, "I can handle this," I can assure you, you can't and you won't.

Growing up on a farm, I learned that a horse can fall into a slough (a miry bog) alone, but he can't get out alone. He has to be pulled out with ropes hitched to a tractor.

No one has to help you become an addict. You can fall into the pit alone. You might say, "I didn't fall. I was pushed." Whether willingly or unwillingly, when you are in a deep pit, you need to be rescued. God comes into the pit with you. He doesn't just throw you a rope. Instead, he says, "I will come into the miry bog where you are. I will scoop you up, put your feet upon a rock, make your steps secure, and put a new song in your mouth."

Jesus came into this dirty world to rescue us. We are worse off than we ever thought. Jesus came to do for us what we can't do for ourselves.

Our Struggle Magnifies Grace

Not too long ago I met two former addicts while on an airplane. Even before the plane took off, I had already struck up a conversation with the one sitting next to me, and he told me his story. He now works for the organization that helped rescue him from drugs and alcohol. I learned that there are about 200 addicts at their facility, and each one is put to work to earn his own money. His friend, who was seated in the row ahead of us, chimed in on our conversation.

"What were you into?" I asked both of them. Basically they had the same story: "It began with marijuana, then it progressed to heroin, alcohol...name it, and I've done it."

True, these men were helped by an organization established to help addicts, but what was the key to their heart-change? The answer is God's grace. These men understand grace much better than the "goody two-shoes" who don't think they need that much grace because, after all, they've lived so uprightly. These men said that the fact that God loved them and accepted them despite their sins and crimes was what motivated them to seek help and accept the accountability they needed. And, although they have been free for about two years, they were aware they could retreat back into darkness if given a tempting opportunity.

Jesus condemned people who thought they didn't need much grace but were content with their own righteousness. But to those who knew their need, He motivated them to seek forgiveness, cleansing, and restoration by His blessed presence. It was the hated tax collector who went home justified, while the self-righteous man retreated back into his unacknowledged darkness (see Luke 18:9-14).

The two former addicts told me they were taught to thank God for His love for them even while they struggled. The assurance that they could come to God and be received and welcomed gave them the security to admit to their need and embrace the healthy relationships that led to a real sense of freedom.

In the book *Redemption: Freed by Jesus from the Idols We Worship and the Wounds We Carry*, Mike Wilkerson writes about his temptation with pornography:

> I remember that many times in those decisive moments—to click or not to click—I felt what seemed like the Holy Spirit tapping me on the shoulder. I knew better than this. I also knew what was better than this; the peace of God's presence was better than a rush from porn. But in that moment, I didn't believe it. I shrugged him off and my body would chill as I reached a trembling hand for the mouse.
>
> God was never less present with me. In fact, he was there convicting me of sin. But...I traded the peace of God to make peace with sin...He had given me a way of escape—his presence—but I ignored him...I had willingly hardened my heart in unbelief...Yet, still, he was there, my way of escape. His presence, finally, was my rescue."[2]

His presence was my rescue!

Of course there were failures along the way, but the issue for this man, and for us, is whether we will avail ourselves of God's grace and take the way of escape. "No temptation has overtaken you that is not common to man. God is faithful, and he will not let you be tempted beyond your ability, but with the temptation he will also provide the way of escape, that you may be able to endure it" (1 Corinthians 10:13).

Only when we value the presence of God more than we do our own flight from reality into the world of our preferred addiction do we find the power to say *no*. Or to put it differently, freedom comes when our passion for God is greater than our passion to sin; this is a lesson we all must learn. It's not just for addicts.

At the church where I serve, we have a special class for men who are seeking freedom from pornography. We call it the 5:8 class based on Matthew 5:8: "Blessed are the pure in heart, for they shall see God." The desire to "see God" and to please Him is a strong motivation to leave the darkness behind.

Run to Jesus, Not Away from Him

This may be the most important lesson we can learn in our quest for a clear conscience. When we sin and are burdened with guilt and remorse, we are tempted to run away from Jesus—to put as much distance as we can between us and the Lord. I've heard people say, "I can't handle the 'God thing' right now. Someday when I get a grip on my life, I will think about God. I'll clean myself up, at least a bit, and then deal with Him." A huge mistake.

A woman who was sexually involved with a man came to me for counsel. Later she told me that her bond with this man was so strong that before she walked into my office, she thought that if I told her to break the relationship she would die.

During the counseling session, I asked her, "Who do you love more: God, or this man?" She thought about that for a moment, and then, mustering all the strength she had, she said, "God." She told me later that she left saying to herself, "I won't die...I will live." And that was the beginning of breaking this sinful relationship whose "soul ties" were so binding, so powerful, and yes, so inviting, and so fulfilling.

Even in the midst of temptation, we need to be reminded of the blood of Christ—that we belong to Him, and that in Christ we are the righteousness of God. We must stand on that in the midst of the temptation until we begin to ask ourselves, "Why am I, as a son or daughter of God, doing what displeases Him?"

We have to be willing to open all the "baggage" we're carrying, and in the presence of Jesus, allow Him to help us put our past behind us and move on to a better future.

During the Protestant Reformation, there was a composer

named Martin Arcola. He was also a teacher in a Protestant school. Arcola wrote, "Though my sins were as great and many as the hairs of my head, the grass of the earth, the leaves of the tree, the sand on the seashore, the drops in the sea, or the stars of heaven, yet I would not fall into despair. But I would run to the great indulgence chest, namely the grace and the overwhelming mercy of God."[3]

Arcola was saying, "Run to Jesus! Run, don't walk!"

At the beginning of John 8, we read about the woman who was caught in adultery. She was dragged to Jesus by men who wanted to find fault with the Man who claimed to forgive sins. These self-righteous religious leaders cared nothing about the woman; rather, they were seeking to trap Jesus: "Teacher, this woman has been caught in the act of adultery. Now in the Law Moses commanded us to stone such women. So what do you say?" (John 8:4-5).

I smile at Jesus Christ's answer. After writing on the ground for a few moments, He stood up and said, "Let him who is without sin among you be the first to throw a stone at her" (verse 7). In other words, "Sure, you keep the Law, and if you haven't committed a similar sin, pick up some stones and start throwing them at her."

Then Jesus bent down and wrote on the ground again to give His words time to burn shame and conviction into the hearts of the woman's accusers.

John continues, "But when they heard it, they went away one by one, beginning with the older ones, and Jesus was left alone with the woman standing before him" (verse 9). They all left, beginning with the older ones, who obviously had a greater load of their own guilt.

And then we read, "Jesus stood up and said to her, 'Woman, where are they? Has no one condemned you?' She said, 'No one, Lord.' And Jesus said, 'Neither do I condemn you; go, and from now on sin no more'" (verses 10-11).

For this woman, being caught in her sin was a gift! And it's the same for every addict who suffers alone. Sharon Hersh, author of *The Last Addiction* speaks about "the great, unspeakable gift of addiction."[4] The adulterous woman in John 8 was absolutely unable to help herself or to break free from her sin. But being exposed in the presence of Jesus was her healing. She was caught, only to be set free.

The scribes and Pharisees (John 8:3) who caught her were also caught. But they walked away from Jesus with their masks of self-righteous deception and conceit fully intact, saying, "We may be guilty of the same thing, but we're not about to admit it and let Jesus set us free!"

What a contrast. The guilty sinner hears the words of Jesus: "Your sins are forgiven. Go and sin no more." The self-righteous stand aloof and say, "We don't have any addictions. None!" So they judge all those who struggle with their sexuality, their addictions, and their failures. The self-righteous are blind to their own needs; they see the speck in someone else's eye with clarity but are blind to the beam in their own.

Jesus is saying to you and me, "If you will come into My presence, even with your baggage of shame, I will enter into your world and bring the deliverance you need."

The two former addicts I met that day on the plane now represent the ministry that helped them out of their addiction. They are proof that, with a clear conscience, it's possible to move out of despair into hope and expectation. They, like the apostle Paul, who at one time had murdered Christians, can join him in saying, "For our boast is this, the testimony of our conscience, that we behaved in the world with simplicity and godly sincerity, not by earthly wisdom but by the grace of God" (2 Corinthians 1:12).

A clear conscience gives us the incentive to serve God with freedom and joy. That is the testimony of forgiven sinners throughout the ages. It can be the testimony of anyone who receives God's grace with honesty and submission.

A Passage to Ponder:

Come to me, all who labor and are heavy laden, and I will give you rest. Take my yoke upon you and learn from me, for I am gentle and lowly in heart, and you will find rest for your souls (Matthew 11:28-29).

Probing Questions to Consider:

Ask yourself: "Am I willing to expose my life to God's grace and the accountability of other believers to break my sin cycle and have the freedom to be what God intends?" If you answer no, then what would God have to do in your life to bring you to that necessary point of desperation? If you answer yes, spend time in prayer now, asking God to help you search your heart and fully yield its desires to Him. Then take time to determine how you can make yourself accountable to both God and others so that you receive the help and encouragement you need to bring about real life change.

6

The Healing Power of Light

There is no pillow so soft as a clear conscience.

FRENCH PROVERB

Back in September of 2012, a TSA agent named Andy Ramirez was caught stealing an iPad from a Florida airport. What Ramirez didn't know was that the iPad he brought home had a tracking device that enabled investigators to locate it. So when they showed up at his doorstep thirty miles from the airport, he was, to say the least, quite surprised. What happened next is very instructive about human nature.

When asked whether he knew where the iPad was, he denied that he had seen it; in fact, he denied it repeatedly. Then, thanks to technology, they were able to set off an alarm and asked him to search his house to find it. A moment later, with his wife standing behind him, he sheepishly gave it to the investigators. When asked how it got from the airport to his house, he did exactly what Adam did when confronted by God in Eden. Incredibly, Ramirez said, "My wife says she brought it home...I don't know where she got it from." You can only guess at the argument that erupted when the investigators left!

When a married man or woman suspects that their mate may be cheating, they sometimes hire detectives to track their partner.

What is fascinating is to see the lengths to which people will lie, manipulate, and use guilt ("You don't trust me!"), and be willing to accuse the whole world if need be to maintain the façade of their innocence. Only when they see the video from a hidden camera do they admit to guilt, and when caught, they attempt to justify themselves or minimize their cheating.

Years ago I had two briefcases—one I used regularly, and another I used whenever I traveled, usually on an airplane. One day, the flight attendants were handing out ham sandwiches sealed in clear wrap. I didn't feel hungry at the moment, but I took one and put it in my briefcase, thinking I would eat it later.

For weeks afterward, whenever I walked into my office (you know where this is going), there was this musty smell, and I couldn't detect where it was coming from. Then when I was getting ready for my next trip, I opened the briefcase, and there was the sandwich. Can you guess what a ham sandwich looks and smells like after it's been at room temperature for a month?

All of us can identify. We've taken our sin, wrapped it, and hidden it, thinking nobody will ever know. But there's always, figuratively speaking, an odor; no matter how well it's hidden, our conscience reminds us that *it is there*. And evidence of it can be seen in our critical attitudes, in our defensiveness, in our shallow relationships, and in our willingness to commit other sins or crimes. That iPad in the closet robs us of peace. Or to put it differently, our conscience reminds us that a rotten sandwich is in our briefcase.

Many people do their best to stifle their conscience; they hope against hope that the twinge of guilt they feel can be unlearned. They have no intention of bringing their sin into the light of day, and because of this, they forfeit the healing that light can bring.

This chapter is an invitation for us to open our closets, admit to the stolen iPads, and make peace with our past. God goes with us into the dark rooms of our life, shining a light, and along with it, He brings a fresh breeze that reminds us of what a clear conscience is like.

Different Kinds of Darkness

Not all who manage their darkness are dishonest; sometimes they may just be concealing memories of childhood abuse and personal pain. A woman whom we shall call Rachel grew up in what appeared to be a fine Christian home. Her father was a well-liked Sunday school teacher. But in secret, he would sexually abuse his daughter and force her to lie in cold water, warning her that if she ever told on him, she would pay the consequences. His harshness was always mingled with the appearance of tenderness about the church and the Bible. He'd ask Rachel to sing hymns for him and would shower her with gifts. This was basically hush money, intended to buy her silence. And, to make matters worse, Rachel's mother appeared to be oblivious as to what was going on. Yet during the night, Rachel's father would come into her bedroom, expecting that they'd engage in various forms of sex.

Eventually Rachel did leave home and, several boyfriends later, she did marry. But she couldn't relate to her husband sexually and found herself depressed and angry. She had determined that no one would ever know about her past. She treated her husband with contempt. Her angry, unfounded accusations against him escalated. Having been sinned against by her father, she, in turn, sinned against her husband.

Finally, when the pain was too great for her to bear, she told her husband the story of her past so that he could understand the root of their conflict. They received counseling and are now managing in their marriage. She's learning, as all of us must, that we must be willing to bring our darkness into the light because darkness never produces light on its own.

The man who has committed adultery has to come to the light

in order to be released from his deceit. Rachel had to come to the light to deal with the evil deeds of her father and the sin against her husband. Although their stories are different, they have this in common: Only the light can heal them.

The premise of this chapter is that, although the truth hurts, lies hurt even more. Therefore we must leave the darkness and come to the light, where there is forgiveness, reconciliation, and healing. Only truth in the presence of God sets us free.

Keep in mind that there are some people who will never come to the light. They are so content with themselves, so self-satisfied, so convinced of their personal righteousness that they see no need for change. They confuse darkness with light, and try to muddle through life as best they can. "The way of the wicked is like deep darkness; they do not know over what they stumble" (Proverbs 4:19).

They keep stumbling, try to pick themselves up and keep walking. They make peace with their emptiness, their failed attempts at happiness, and their failed relationships. The thought of coming into the light is fearful.

Coming into the Light

Jesus put it this way: "This is the judgment: the light has come into the world, and people loved the darkness rather than the light because their works were evil. For everyone who does wicked things hates the light and does not come to the light, lest his works should be exposed. But whoever does what is true comes to the light, so that it may be clearly seen that his works have been carried out in God" (John 3:19-21).

What a difference light makes!

A businessman called his pastor, sobbing on the phone, asking him to come over immediately. When the pastor arrived at the man's office, he was slumped over his desk, sobbing so violently that he was unable to speak. The pastor thought for certain that the man's wife had died, or perhaps a child. But when the man was able to regain his composure, he said, "God has just shown me my heart, and it was as if I was looking into the pit of hell."

What sin had this man committed? Murder? Adultery? Grand theft? No, he had, however, falsified some expense accounts while doing business for his company. The total amount was quite small, perhaps a few hundred dollars over a period of years. Most businessmen would think nothing of it; such minor infractions are done all the time. This man's sin was small in comparison to that of others. Small, that is, *until he saw God!*

In the presence of the Almighty, all rationalizations fade into oblivion; no sin is minor; every infraction is "a big deal." Only when we compare ourselves with ourselves do we think that our sins are not too serious. But in the presence of God, we see ourselves as we are, not how we wish we were. One difference between superficial repentance and genuine repentance is that the first is based on being discovered by men, the second is based on being "discovered" by God.

Resistance to Light

Back on the farm we had a musty basement that we dared not enter without a flashlight. The moment the light shone, the bugs would scurry between the cracks, under the debris. These vermin could find contentment only in darkness. Just so, we often find darkness to be a safe retreat, a place where we can go without risking the shame of exposure.

As a general rule, we can say that the greater our sin, the more resistance we have to the light. Martin Buber, in his writings, referred to "the uncanny game of hide-and-seek in the obscurity of the soul, in which it, the single human soul, evades itself, avoids itself, hides from itself."[1]

Whatever pain walking in the light brings, the healing it brings is worth the price. For in the light, my false self is exposed, I admit who I am, and I experience God's indescribable grace. Either I cry to God for mercy for my sin, or I turn away from the light, determined to stay in the safety of darkness.

Light Reveals Our True Selves

Walk away from a street lamp, and you will notice your shadow becoming longer—so long, in fact, that it will eventually fade into the distance. But as you come closer to the light, your shadow will become shorter until there is none at all. Mark it well: If we want to take a true measure of ourselves, we must come into the light of God's presence through His Word. There we will not measure ourselves by our achievements, nor by the opinions of those around us, not even by the opinions of ourselves. There we are in the presence of the One who knows us and loves us. "For at one time you were darkness, but now you are light in the Lord. Walk as children of light" (Ephesians 5:8).

Let's remind ourselves that those who have seen a revelation of God have always been humbled, devastated by the depth of their sinfulness. Remember when Job was upset with the Almighty, blaming Him for the seemingly unjust calamities he was suffering? But when Job saw God, he said, "Behold, I am of small account; what shall I answer you? I lay my hand on my mouth. I have spoken once, and I will not answer; twice, but I will proceed no further...I had heard of you by the hearing of the ear, but now my eye sees you; therefore I despise myself, and repent in dust and ashes" (Job 40:4-5; 42:5-6).

Isaiah had a vision of God and declared, "Woe is me! For I am lost; for I am a man of unclean lips, and I dwell in the midst of a people of unclean lips; for my eyes have seen the King, the Lord of hosts!" (Isaiah 6:5). Peter, recognizing Jesus to be the Christ said,

"Depart from me, for I am a sinful man, O Lord" (Luke 5:8). No one can approach the light without being keenly aware that darkness resides in the human heart.

If I continue to deny the dark side of me—the part that seems so unlovable—then I can't walk in the light. For light cannot shine where there's dishonesty. "If we say we have fellowship with him while we walk in darkness, we lie and do not practice the truth" (1 John 1:6). And if I confess the darkness that I know about, God will graciously forgive the darkness of which I am not aware. That, I believe, is what John meant when he wrote, "If we walk in the light, as he is in the light, we have fellowship with one another, and the blood of Jesus his Son cleanses us from all sin" (1 John 1:7).

"It is the nature of the false self" wrote James Masterson, "to save us from knowing the truth about our real selves, from penetrating the deeper causes of our unhappiness, from seeing ourselves as we really are—vulnerable, afraid, terrified, and unable to let our real selves emerge."[2] Keep in mind that a surgeon cuts, but only in order to heal. The pain brings gain, the wounds turn into scars, and the false turns into truth. Light not only *reveals*, it also *heals*.

Light Leads to Honest Confession

Let's review who God is. "This is the message we have heard from him and proclaim to you, that God is light, and in him is no darkness at all" (1 John 1:5). God is pure light, pure reality, pure brilliance, and pure holiness. His light is such that He is intolerant of sin. He hates impurity and sin because there is no darkness in Him—none at all.

By now you might be saying, "How does this help me have a clear conscience? His holiness makes me want to run and hide."

Stay with me here.

Yes, God is pure, uncreated light. So how do we bridge the gap between God and us, between pure light and total darkness? We know that God is not going to compromise His holiness; He is the light and will always be light.

Thanks to Jesus, John was able to write this to Christians: "If we confess our sins, he is faithful and just to forgive us our sins and to cleanse us from all unrighteousness" (1 John 1:9).

John began, "If we confess our sins." The word "confess" here means to agree with God. Literally, in the original Greek text, it means "to say the same thing" as God. When we confess our sins, we need to confess them individually. We should confess whatever sins God brings to our consciousness. God requires that we admit to the sins that He brings to our attention. Confession is a spiritual discipline that restores our fellowship with God.

A story comes to us from a primitive culture about a woman who took all of her dirty clothes, wrapped them in a bundle, and took them to the river to be cleaned. There were other women present who were washing their clothes, but this woman was so embarrassed because her clothes were so tattered and dirty that all she did was dip the bundle into the river several times and take it back home.

That's the way some Christians confess their sins. "Okay, God, I've messed up." Anybody who confesses his sins in that manner is not really confessing his sins because there's a second part to confession. It's not merely that we agree with God that our sin is wrong. We must also agree with Him that He has the right to take this out of our lives forever, and we invite Him to get rid of this sin that we are confessing.

Confession is like repentance. It is a yieldedness to God, saying, "God, whatever You say, I'm agreeing with You, and I confess my sins individually, one by one, as You bring them to my attention. And I also agree that these sins have got to go out of my life."

So confession is not just vaguely saying, "God, forgive my sins," but "God, I am cheating my company. Forgive me." And then we must continue: "And God, help me to know how to make this right, because I can't continue living with this condemning conscience. I agree with You about everything."

Or "I'm lying to my husband; You have to help me get out of this web of lies and remove all deception." This is a prayer of submission. "I agree with You, Lord."

Or "I agree, Lord, that I am involved in an unholy sexual relationship. I've tried to justify it a hundred different ways, but I want to worship You. I'm agreeing with You that what I'm doing is sin, but I'm also agreeing with You that You have the right to end this relationship forever. By Your grace I will follow through with my decision to be honest about my behavior."

In the Light We Accept Forgiveness

After confession comes the promise of 1 John 1:9 that "He is faithful and just to forgive us our sins." We can claim our forgiveness because God is trustworthy. What He says is true. It's in the Word; we are to believe it and receive it.

A woman said to me, "Pastor Lutzer, I had an abortion, and the little girl would be about three years old now if I hadn't aborted her. When I walk into a mall and I see a girl who is about that age, I'm just absolutely overwhelmed with guilt."

I asked her, "Did you confess your sin?"

"I've confessed it a thousand times," she replied.

Out of her deep pain and regret, this dear mother is really saying, "God is *not* faithful and just to forgive us our sins." She is caught in a cycle of confession, guilt, confession, guilt, and so on. That's why the last phrase of 1 John 1:9 is so important. When we confess our sins, God is faithful and just to forgive them, "and to cleanse us from all unrighteousness."

The woman needed to not only accept God's forgiveness, but also His *cleansing*—His subjective work done in the human heart.

She didn't need to wallow in the past each time she saw a little three-year-old girl. In doing so, she was acting as if God isn't righteous and faithful to forgive her. She needed to affirm God's promise to forgive: "Lord, thank You for Your forgiveness; I thank You that my sin has lost its power over me. I'm going to give You praise because this sin no longer stands between You and me, and I receive that."

Like David, who famously committed adultery with Bathsheba, she must affirm, "Blessed is the one whose transgression is forgiven, whose sin is covered. Blessed is the man against whom the LORD counts no iniquity, and in whose spirit there is no deceit" (Psalm 32:1-2).

When we confess our sins, God throws them into the depths of the sea (see Micah 7:19) and then puts up a sign that says, "No fishing!" God told Israel that based on His new covenant with them, He could say, "I will forgive their iniquity, and I will remember their sin no more" (Jeremiah 31:34).

Now, what about the sins we've forgotten about, or what if we've done something that we don't even view as sin, but God might see it as such? Here's good news: If we are walking in the light of God and keeping in fellowship with Him, God forgives us even for those sins that we've forgotten or may be unaware of. We are cleansed from these sins so that fellowship with God is not only possible, but enjoyable.

The Light Enables Us to Enjoy God

Please don't hurry over this!

What I'm about to share with you is so astonishing that you will find it difficult to believe. Let's review these words: "If we walk in the light, as he is in the light, we have fellowship with one another, and the blood of Jesus his Son cleanses us from all sin" (1 John 1:7).

Your first response might be yes, we have fellowship with other Christians, and of course that is true. But as we take a closer look at this verse, we notice that the antecedent (remember your grade school grammar?) of the phrase "we have fellowship with one another" is not other Christians, but God Himself. In other words *we have fellowship with God, and God has fellowship with us!*

Let me say it again: God desires fellowship with us! But He can't have fellowship with us as long as we cower in darkness. We have to unpack our baggage in the light of His grace and forgiveness. To have fellowship with God, we must live exposed to the light.

The High Cost of Coming to the Light

What price are you willing to pay to have a conscience that is clear before God and others? Unfortunately, the frown of our friends often means more to us than the smile of God. We must overcome our natural inclination to hide our shame and come to the light, no matter what the cost. The false self, that part of us that denies greed and self-centeredness and sinful acts, can never be healed without exposure. That part of us that draws significance from achievements and the adulation of others, that part of us that withdraws from those who are a threat to us, that part of us that judges others for sins of which we are guilty, that part of us must be brought to the light. When the false self is exposed, and we know we are radically loved by God, we are truly set free. Brennan Manning quotes Barbara Finand: "Wholeness is brokenness owned and thereby healed."[3]

In the early 1970s, a great revival swept Western Canada. This revival caught the attention of the secular press because of all the people who were making things right in their lives. The Canadian equivalent of the IRS (Internal Revenue Service) was receiving checks from people who wanted to make up for cheating on their past income tax forms.

My sister-in-law went back to a store to pay for a 99-cent bag of potatoes that was on the bottom of her shopping cart and was accidentally overlooked at the checkout. When she went to the store manager and confessed, he said, "Either it's my lucky day, or something is happening in this town. You're the second person who has come to me today to confess theft."

I am reminded of the man who taught me chemistry in high school. He was in church as often as the pews. He and his family were there all the time. He taught Sunday school and was in a leadership position in the church. But years earlier, this man had cheated on a term paper while studying for his master's degree. From our standpoint, we would say it wasn't that big of a deal. But he said that when he walked across the stage to receive his degree, it was as if his feet were as heavy as lead. His conscience troubled him so greatly that he returned to the University, willing to hand in his degree. They did not accept it, but he was willing to pay the price.

For some, the cost of coming to the light is monetary. A Christian contractor had cheated his clients by putting inferior materials in the houses he built. In short, he promised them one quality of boards, insulation, and the like, but gave them another. When he tried to be honest in the presence of God, he could not escape his dishonesty and thievery. No matter how he rationalized it, no matter how often he confessed his sin to God, he knew that he could never be at peace as long as restitution was within his power. When he finally did what he knew he should, he went to the bank and borrowed money to repay his customers. "Fellowship with God has cost me thousands of dollars," he told me, "but it is worth every penny."

On the morning of December 21, 1975, fourteen-year-old John Claypool shot and killed his neighbor and his wife for no reason other than to feel what it was like to see someone die. Though the police questioned him and he was the prime suspect, he was let go for lack of direct evidence. He later admitted that his sinister deed lived on in his mind. He told no one about it, and planned to take his secret to the grave.

Eventually he married, had two children, and then his wife left him. God brought some Christians into his life and he yearned for the peace they had. "This yearning for peace with God was driven by the constant weight that I felt in my soul from my sin." He purchased a Bible and realized that Jesus could save him from his sins. He was converted. Then his heart pounded in fear as the Holy Spirit seemed to say to him, "My child, you must obey Me by confessing your crime or you will never know My full blessing on your life."

He told the woman he was dating at the time about his dark secret, and she broke up with him. Finally, on November 27, 1995, with the help of his pastor and an attorney, John surrendered to the authorities. While great fear gripped him as his deceit was exposed by the media, he said:

> Yet God was faithful to his promise to uphold me. At the moment of truth, though I was now a prisoner of the law, I was set free before God for the first time in my life. I cannot describe the feeling of that burden completely lifted—the Lord now held his once-disobedient child in His loving arms; and true to His promise, He did not let me fall! A wonderful peace came over my soul, such as I had never known before...
>
> I am now confined in a maximum-security prison, serving time for second-degree murder. But I am more free and more at peace than at any other time in my life.[4]

In contrast, a Christian man who falsified an application form for workman's compensation would not come to the light, though his pastor told him he should. He sustained an injury on a vacation that he reported as having happened on the job. He now receives a monthly paycheck and will do so till he dies. He said, "Do you think that I am going to confess to the compensation board? I'd go to jail for it. Sorry, but I want to keep things the way they are." He doesn't realize it would be better to be in fellowship with God in jail than walking in darkness as a "free" man.

Coming to the light is always worth it, not just to clear your conscience, but to have a satisfying relationship with God. In His presence we are healed.

Transforming Lessons

Let's remember these lessons as we think about coming to the light.

1. What we hide hurts.

There's some truth to the statement that you are only as sick as your darkest secrets. That's true for the person who has sinned as well as the person who has been sinned against. Those who have been the victims of injustice and now are vindictive toward others must also come to the light.

Of course "coming to the light" means different things for different people. For all of us it means honesty before God, a humble facing of our thoughts, desires, and actions no matter how shameful they might be. For others, it means the need to be reconciled to others (see chapter 9), or the need to be counseled and affirmed by those you trust. Remember, the purpose is not simply to expose the darkness, but to enjoy the light.

2. Light and darkness cannot coexist.

There's a legend in which the sun, speaking to a dark cave, says, "Why don't you come up into the light?" The dark cave accepts the suggestion and brings itself into the light and says, "Now I've experienced some light. Sun, why don't you come into my cave so that you can experience some darkness?"

The sun accepted the offer, and as it descended into the cave it said, "I don't see any darkness here at all." When darkness and light collide, light always wins.

When we see light, we must either move toward it or move back into the darkness. If we choose to retreat into the darkness, our hearts will become a little harder and we'll become more comfortable with the darkness. This is what happens to those whom Paul described as having a hardened conscience, cauterized by indifference to the light of God (see 1 Timothy 4:2). We should not be surprised that among the truly evil are some who, at one time, appeared to walk in the light. For the greater the light we reject, the greater the darkness we must embrace.

3. The question is not whether we have come to the light, but whether we are now walking in it.

Sometimes when someone falls into sin—immorality for example—we ask, "Did he repent?" But actually the better question would be, "Is he repenting?" The person who has come to the light in the past might be walking in darkness today. Coming into the light is only the first step in the journey. The fact is that every believer should be walking in greater light today than he did yesterday. Life is a journey and only becomes a destination at death.

Can a Christian who has walked in the light return to darkness? Yes. As we've already learned, "If *we* claim to have fellowship with him yet walk in the darkness, *we* lie and do not live out the truth" (1 John 1:6 NIV, emphasis added). We prove our love for God by walking in the light despite the cost.

Let me give you the best advice you might read in this book: When your conscience has been cleared by confession, keep your account with God and others *current*! Confess your sin to God the moment you become aware of it; don't let sins pile up with the intention of dealing with them later. Your goal should be constant fellowship with God and with others. No more postponing; no more hiding.

Getting Found

Robert Fulghum, in *All I Really Needed to Know I Learned in Kindergarten,* told how one October when he was a child, he and his friends would play hide-and-seek under piles of fallen leaves. There was one kid who always hid so well that nobody could find him. Eventually, the others gave up searching for him. When he finally showed up, they would explain that there is hiding and there is finding, and he was not to hide in such a way that he could not be found.

Fulghum continues:

> As I write this, the neighborhood game goes on, and there is a kid under a pile of leaves in the yard just under my window. He has been there a long time now, and everybody else is found and they are about to give up on him over at the base. I considered going out to the base and telling them where he is hiding. And I thought about setting the leaves on fire to drive him out. Finally, I just yelled, "GET FOUND, KID!" out the window. And it scared him so bad he probably...started crying and ran home to tell his mother. It is real hard to know how to be helpful sometimes. [5]

You may be playing hide-and-seek grown-up style. You may be trying to hide so well you'll never be found. We've all hidden under piles of leaves so skillfully arranged that no one can see us. At first, we congratulate ourselves, for there is a sense of security in knowing that no one can find us. But eventually God turns our hiding place into a private hell. And then we want to be found out no matter what the cost.

"Search me, O God, and know my heart! Try me and know my thoughts! And see if there be any grievous way in me, and lead me in the way everlasting!" (Psalm 139:23-24). So I shout to you under your pile of rationalizations, under your pile of bitterness, under your pile of deception: GET FOUND!

A Passage to Ponder:

This is the message we have heard from him and proclaim to you, that God is light, and in him is no darkness at all. If we say we have fellowship with him while we walk in darkness, we lie and do not practice the truth. But if we walk in the light, as he is in the light, we have fellowship with one another, and the blood of Jesus his Son cleanses us from all sin. If we say we have no sin, we deceive ourselves, and the truth is not in us (1 John 1:5-8).

Probing Questions to Consider:

Do an honest inventory of your life, asking yourself: What closets of darkness have I not exposed to God? Invite the Holy Spirit to help you open those doors and uncover those matters you have been trying to hide from yourself and others. Determine to walk in the light each day and not allow sins to pile up. Instead, confess them whenever they are brought to your attention.

Conflicts of Conscience

*The testimony of a good conscience is worth more
than a dozen character witnesses.*

AUTHOR UNKNOWN

I am even crying writing to you. My daughters and I are very modest but I let them wear baggy shorts and pants for gym in the public school. We don't always follow the dress code of our church: long sleeves—skirts, very long hair is a must. And my husband is okay with me and our daughters not conforming to these expectations. But the leadership at the church we attend say that we are backslidden and lost."

She continues, "My conscience bothers me when these people visit...I am in bondage. Am I worldly to want to look pretty with simplicity? Why can't I let this dress issue go? Why do I worry about what they think? Am I condemned? Am I not walking in the light? Am I lost? The enemy has used this on me for years. I don't want to miss heaven for trying to look nice."

My response is to say that yes, most assuredly women should be modest, but to expect women to conform to certain standards such as she has described puts the emphasis in the wrong place. Even the Old Testament prohibition that a woman should not wear the garments of a man has more to do with cross-dressing than it does with whether a woman wears a pantsuit or a skirt. Nor is it wrong for a woman to look beautiful. Of course, in our culture, beauty is often overrated. The television shows and other media that emphasize beauty and sexuality are destroying our young people.

But how can this woman be delivered from the harsh legalism of her church? Jesus, it seems to me, would admonish us to focus on the heart and not whether some rather petty rules are kept. Sometimes it might simply be best to not join a church where members are required to meet certain arbitrary standards.

How should these disputes be resolved?

The New Testament teaches that sometimes Christians disagree about matters of conduct because one person's conscience might allow them to do something that another's conscience would forbid them to do. We have to learn to be careful in judging one another.

We must never forget that some things are always wrong: It's always wrong to break the commandments; it's always wrong to be conformed to the world; it's always wrong to permit unwholesome words to proceed out of our mouths; it's always wrong to grieve the Holy Spirit; it's always wrong to feed our sensual appetites. The list could go on.

On the other hand, there are some things that are always right: It's always right to love one another; it's always right to set our affection on things above, not on things of the earth; it's always right to be filled with the Spirit; it's always right to be honest and to respect other people.

However, there are some matters that are difficult to classify categorically as either right or wrong, sinful or not. Some things are a matter of conscience. In Europe, for example, Christians routinely drink wine or other fermented drinks; they're surprised that many Christians in the United States believe in total abstinence. Many of us argue that given the curse of alcoholism, it's better to not take a single drink. But others counter that anything—including food—can be misused. In biblical times, Jesus took water and turned it into wine. So the disagreements continue.

There was a time when we heard from the pulpits in our country that no Christian should ever attend a theater. Yet today, for good or ill, Christians do so routinely. There was a time when Christians never participated in Sunday sports, yet today we honor Christian athletes even if their schedules don't allow them to attend church during the playing season. The list of dos and don'ts varies from culture to culture and from one era to another.

How do we resolve these differences?

I'm well aware that by discussing these matters, I'm walking through a minefield. The most distinctive characteristic of a minefield is that the mines are hidden. I'm taking the risk of stepping on one unexpectedly, but we have to remember that one man's minefield is another's protection. So let's walk through this chapter together.

All of us are tempted to universalize our personal convictions; we want to absolutize that which should be relative. We think that because we like a certain kind of music that everyone should enjoy that same kind of music. Some Christians say, "God hates the same worship music I do!" We would be shocked at how differently Christians worship in other parts of the world; some are reserved, and others worship with freedom in singing and dance. We are locked into our own culture much more than we realize, yet we always want to absolutize our personal preferences.

The other temptation is to relativize sin. There is a tendency to make sin acceptable by reducing absolutes to cultural norms and perspectives. When we do that, we lower the standards rather than rooting them in sound biblical principles. We should always be trying to find the balance between the dangers of legalism and the dangers of license.

A third problem is that we tend to define spirituality in terms of what we don't do. We like lists of dos and don'ts because they help us define the content of Christian living. Some of us remember the oft-used lingo, "Don't drink, dance, or chew, or go around with girls who do!" Some people still think that proof of conversion is simply to live with the right "rules." And for some churches, those rules mean that women can't wear pants to the gym or even in winter.

Are those who keep rules—even strict rules—legalistic? Perhaps, and perhaps not. Legalism is the wrong use of laws or rules. If I keep certain rules thinking that they make me godly, then yes, I am legalistic. Rules can keep me from certain select sins; but what rules can't do is give me righteousness. Rules do not cause me to love God or to strive for holiness. Jesus tried to get the Pharisees to realize that rules can't change the heart.

Here in Chicago, there's a section of the city with 160,000 inhabitants. Not a single one drinks a drop of liquor, or smokes, or dances, or goes to movies. I mentioned that to a friend, and he said that he'd really like to visit this section of the city, maybe even move there. I told him that someday, that might be possible. The area of the city, however, is Rosehill Cemetery! You see, some who define the Christian life by what they *don't* do are missing the point.

But rules—even the negative ones—do have some value. I grew up with rules that kept me from certain sins, and we raised our children with many of the same standards. There are many things that are not wise to do; other things are downright wrong. Obviously God put value on the "Thou Shalt Nots," as the Ten Commandments remind us.

So we shouldn't be critical of those who keep certain rules. They might be legalistic, but not necessarily. Jesus didn't mind the Pharisees keeping their rules (though some of those rules went beyond the bounds of Scripture), but He grieved over the fact that they stopped short of developing intimacy with God.

To recap: Two people can keep the same rules, yet one can do so legalistically because he believes that the rules define his relationship with God, while the other does so knowing that the important thing is to cultivate his relationship with God. At root, legalism is a matter of heart and motive.

To some readers, this chapter will appear to deal with trivial matters. But when you're a member of the family of God and you want to please the Lord, even trivial issues are important. We have to please the Lord and work with one another—and that's no small task. Thus, we turn to the Bible to discuss the dos and don'ts, and hope that we can agree on the principles, if not the specific conduct. Above all, we do want to live with a clear conscience.

Dos and Don'ts

In first-century Rome, some of the people who were converted to Christianity came from a Jewish heritage, while others came from paganism. Some of the converts were convinced that the dietary laws of the Old Testament should be kept; others accepted the new revelation that such requirements were a thing of the past. Paul wrote to give people principles and clarifications that are still relevant for us today. He tells us that, at times, there can be two legitimate viewpoints, and that we must accept one another and get along.

Here are the guidelines in judging such issues:

Don't Judge One Another

"As for the one who is weak in faith, welcome him, but not to quarrel over opinions. One person believes he may eat anything, while the weak person eats only vegetables" (Romans 14:1-2). How is this to be resolved? Paul continued, "Let not the one who eats despise the one who abstains, and let not the one who abstains pass judgment on the one who eats, for God has welcomed him" (verse 3). Those who understood God's new revelation of freedom from dietary laws (that is, those who were strong) were not to judge those who did not feel free to eat meat (the weak).

Paul regarded those who had freedom in this matter as the strong; those who felt they had to obey the ancient rules were the weak. If we'd been there, we might have seen this quite differently. We probably would have said that the person who adhered to the old Jewish standards was the strong person and the one who had freedom to eat anything was the weak Christian. We tacitly assume that the Christian who has the liberty to enjoy certain activities is weak, while the strong realizes that such freedom is capitulation to the world.

Paul said the opposite is true. A strong Christian will see that morally neutral activities should not be categorically forbidden. A weak Christian will multiply taboos, thinking that spiritual living means conforming to the right set of "don'ts." In Rome, the strong Christians could eat meat with a clear conscience; the weak Christians could not.

Paul's point was that neither the weak nor the strong should judge each other. If a person considers himself strong, he won't judge someone who's weak. The person who goes to the theater should not judge the one who refuses to go; but the one who refuses to go should not judge the one who goes—unless of course, we are talking about a risqué movie that no Christian should see. The point is that the theater itself is neutral; therefore, there has to be latitude without judging. The strong brother sees that the theater in itself is nothing, but he shouldn't judge the weaker brother who believes his presence there would be a compromise with the world.

Let us suppose that you, along with a number of others, were servants in a household. Would it be your responsibility to judge the performance of one of your peers? No. Paul wrote, "Who are you to pass judgment on the servant of another? It is before his own master that he stands or falls. And he will be upheld, for the Lord is able to make him stand" (verse 4). Then Paul went on to illustrate his point by talking about the Sabbath.

After the Jews were saved, some of them couldn't break the habit of observing the seventh day of the week rather than the first day (Sunday). What was Paul's response? "One person esteems one day as better than another, while another esteems all days alike. Each one should be fully convinced in his own mind" (verse 5).

Can a Christian go to a football game on Sunday? If we say, "well, it is fine to *watch* football on television, but we should not *attend* a game on Sunday," then we'll be caught in a host of hairsplitting distinctions. The question is actually one of individual conscience, and we must not judge others regarding the matter. Our Master might permit one of His children to participate and not another. Before your own Master you stand or fall.

Should we not be concerned about how Sunday is being devalued because of sports, shopping, and traveling? Yes, we should be concerned, for although we worship God each day, Sunday is a special time when we gather with the people of God. But the answer is not to make a rule that fits every Christian! The answer is to teach people to love God more than they love sports. And to love the people of God more than they love shopping, or whatever.

Paul would say that whichever day we choose, whether it's Saturday or Sunday, make that our special day; and whatever diet we adopt, we must eat and worship for the glory of God. Let's make sure we have the right motivation, and not be more concerned about judging each other. On matters like these, there is room for differences in the household of God.

The pastor who tells his parishioners that women who wear slacks have lost their salvation and are going to hell is judging his brothers and sisters. Before their own master they will stand or fall. Paul warns us that we will all individually give an account to God. We have to be careful about universalizing our own convictions about such matters.

Don't Cause a Brother or Sister to Stumble

"Therefor let us not pass judgment on one another any longer, but rather decide never to put a stumbling block or hindrance in the way of a brother" (verse 13). Paul repeated this even more clearly a few verses later: "Do not, for the sake of food, destroy the work of God. Everything is indeed clean, but it is wrong for anyone to make another stumble by what he eats. It is good not to eat meat or drink wine or do anything that causes your brother to stumble" (verses 20-21).

What does it mean to put a stumbling block in your brother's way?

Let us consider a slightly different controversy that Paul confronted in the church in Corinth. This city was a center of pagan worship and sexual permissiveness. Part of the pagan worship included eating meat offered to the gods. The priest would take the meat brought by worshippers and put it on the altar. Later, that meat was taken to the marketplace and sold for less than a comparable cut that had come directly from the slaughterhouse. When some of the pagans became Christians, they realized that because idols were nothing, the meat offered to them was not polluted in any way. But there were some Christians who were weak in the faith and who felt that if they ate the meat which had been offered to those deities, they could become entangled again in their past idolatry. They feared that to eat the meat would be to defile themselves.

You can imagine the disagreements.

"I can't believe that you'd eat meat that was offered to Zeus."

"Wait now...who is Zeus? He is nothing; just an idol of stone."

"Yes, but behind those idols are demons."

"Yes, I grant that, but because I am a follower of Jesus, He takes what belonged to the pagan gods and sanctifies it."

One Christian accused the other of lack of separation from the world; the other replied that such an accusation was nothing but narrow-mindedness. Paul said that Christians have liberty on this issue, but that doesn't necessarily mean that Christians should exercise this liberty even if they have proper knowledge (that is, the understanding that an idol is nothing). The fact that some believers knew they could eat such meat didn't mean that they *should* eat the meat. Admittedly, God had declared all foods clean, but because some Christians believed that eating such meat was a concession to paganism, Paul wrote, "Take care that this right of yours does not somehow become a stumbling block to the weak" (1 Corinthians 8:9).

Now, that doesn't mean that we should never do anything that another Christian doesn't like! Christ frequently said and did things that caused offense—even to His own disciples. If He'd been concerned about offending the Pharisees, He wouldn't have healed people on the Sabbath, nor would He have eaten with publicans and sinners. These actions raised the ire of the religious cliques beyond measure, but He did them anyway.

For Paul, being a stumbling block meant *to do something that would make a brother or sister fall back into their former sinful life.* Imagine that a weaker brother is invited to the home of a stronger brother who serves meat. The weaker brother asks whether the meat had been offered to idols, and the stronger brother says, "Yes, it was." This causes the weaker one to believe he's being drawn back to his former associations with pagan gods. The one brother has put the other brother in a predicament where he must either be impolite or violate his conscience. Paul says don't do that.

Although the illustration I'm about to share may seem trivial, I tell it because I was a personal witness to it. A man who spent all of his spare time gambling and drinking in a pool hall was soundly converted. Months later, he was invited into the home of a Christian couple who had a pool table in their basement. The new Christian gasped when he saw the table; he couldn't believe that Christians would play that game, which in his mind, was so sinful. The older Christian man was surprised at the reaction of his new friend. What could possibly be wrong with playing pool? The answer of course, is nothing. But the homeowner would be sinning if he were to insist that his guest play the game. In fact, it would be better to not play the game at all than to force his brother to compromise his convictions.

If drinking wine tempts my brother to return to alcoholism, or if inviting him to a football game revives in him the obsession he once had for sports, or if attending a theater leads him back to his life of sensual pleasure, then I shouldn't do these things even if I have freedom to do so. "Therefore, if food makes my brother stumble, I will never eat meat, lest I make my brother stumble" (1 Corinthians 8:13).

Here's a dictum to live by: *Are we doing anything which, if others were to do, they might be drawn away into sensuality or other forms of sin?*

Don't Violate Your Conscience

Paul continues his instructions to the church at Rome with this exhortation: "The faith that you have, keep between yourself and God. Blessed is the one who has no reason to pass judgment on himself for what he approves. But whoever has doubts is condemned if he eats, because the eating is not from faith. For whatever does not proceed from faith is sin" (Romans 14:22-23). This principle applies equally to the weak and the strong. The weak brother shouldn't do anything that he can't do in faith, even if it's a harmless activity. Nor should the strong brother do something that he doesn't believe is right and good for him. If it violates your conscience, *don't do it.*

Because the conscience is tempered by environment, some people might feel convicted about what are trivial things. Within time, they may begin to accept God's revelation regarding Christian liberty on a particular point. Until that happens, such are sinning if they can't do these things with a clear conscience. And the stronger brother should not have a clear conscience if he's causing another believer to stumble.

For example, there are certain card games that have their origin in occultism. I personally don't play any card games, and I, for one, wouldn't want to play games with occult symbols or associations. That's my deep conviction, so if I played, I'd violate my conscience. However, when I walked into a Christian retirement center, I noticed that many of the people were playing these card games. My first reaction was to judge them and say that no Christian should play these games; and furthermore, they are a waste of time. Think of what could be accomplished if each retiree were to take an interest in missionaries, write them letters, and pray for their children!

Yet upon further thought, I realized I needed to allow for individual conscience. Just as meat offered to idols was sanctified by the Word of God and prayer, so card games in the hands of Christians might be nothing more than that—cards with pictures and no wrongful associations. As Paul said, "Why do you pass judgment on your brother? Or you, why do you despise your brother? For we will all stand before the judgment seat of God...So then each of us will give an account of himself to God" (verses 10-12).

Yes, as we have learned, there are times when we must judge, but let us be sure to judge ourselves first. And, let us make sure that we do not violate our consciences.

Don't Serve Self, But God

In Romans 15, Paul gives us the fourth principle we must follow: "May the God of endurance and encouragement grant you to live in such harmony with one another, in accord with Christ Jesus, that together you may with one voice glorify the God and Father of our Lord Jesus Christ. Therefore welcome one another as Christ has welcomed you, for the glory of God" (verses 5-7).

To live a life that glorifies God means that we transcend the rules; such a motivation transcends the legalist who wants the Christian life reduced to a series of dos and don'ts. It transcends the self-righteous Christian whose freedom has led to license. Here's a principle that exposes our hearts and becomes the basis for all conduct.

You tell me that you have the freedom to attend a theater? If you do, make sure that you attend only those movies that will help you to glorify God. You have the freedom to watch television? You had best watch only those programs that will help you glorify God. If you tell me that you have the freedom to drink wine, make sure to do it to the glory of God—don't let it lead to drunkenness. If you tell me that you have the freedom to play professional sports on Sunday, you had best do it to the glory of God and have the willpower to change your vocation if it interferes with pleasing the One who redeemed you. You say that you, as a woman, have the freedom to dress beautifully? Be sure that you do it for the glory of God.

You have the freedom to use the Internet? Use it to glorify God and switch it off before you're distracted by websites that will lead you astray into pornography or other forms of sensuality. It is the Lord we serve.

Consider the example you are setting for others: "We who are strong have an obligation to bear with the failings of the weak, and not to please ourselves. Let each of us please his neighbor for his good, to build him up. For Christ did not please himself, but as it is written, 'The reproaches of those who reproached you fell on me'" (15:1-3).

Remember, Even Christ Did Not Please Himself!

Clearly, when we live by this standard, we learn that Christianity is not a matter of rules, but *relationship*. The dos and don'ts are only the first steps in learning that some things are wrong. The closer we live to the Lord, the more we realize that even neutral activities become sin when they occupy time and energy that could be used for eternal values. Once we grasp this concept, we will be more and more hesitant to judge others because we see our own failures and sins more clearly.

Finally, if we truly lived by this principle, we would see the total impossibility of living the Christian life in our own power! God's desire for purity would loom so large that we would be driven to Him for supernatural ability. Petty distinctions would pale in comparison to the weightier matters of honesty, a deep affection for God, and the fruit of the Spirit. We would feel helpless, morally weak, and inadequate. We would have a new perspective that would make dependence upon God a necessity for living the Christian life.

Christ hasn't trapped us into being good while others can have a good time! His restrictions were given to us to show us more keenly our need of Him—it's our *relationship* with Him that matters. A Christian is much more than a sinner minus his sins. No wonder Jesus said that He came to give us life and to give it abundantly (see John 10:10).

"In your hearts honor Christ the Lord as holy, always being

prepared to make a defense to anyone who asks you for a reason for the hope that is in you; yet do it with gentleness and respect, *having a good conscience,* so that, when you are slandered, those who revile your good behavior in Christ may be put to shame" (1 Peter 3:15-16, emphasis added).

If we were arrested for being a Christian, would there be enough evidence to convict us? That should help us better determine the prerequisites for genuine Christian conduct!

A Passage to Ponder:

Why do you pass judgment on your brother? Or you, why do you despise your brother? For we will all stand before the judgment seat of God; for it is written,

"As I live, says the Lord, every knee shall bow to me, and every tongue shall confess to God."

So then each of us will give an account of himself to God. Therefore let us not pass judgment on one another any longer, but rather decide never to put a stumbling block or hindrance in the way of a brother. (Romans 14:10-13).

Probing Questions to Consider:

Are you causing others to stumble? Is there anything that you do publicly or privately, which, if someone else were to do, would lead them into sin? What steps of obedience will you take in order to become the kind of example you should be? (Review Romans 14:22-23).

8

Becoming That Impossible Person

From where I'm sitting, I AM the centre of the Universe!

Sebastyne Young

There's a story, apocryphal to be sure, about a man who went to his pastor and said, "My wife is trying to poison me."

The pastor said, "No, wait! I know your wife. She's a nice woman. There's no way she'd try to poison you."

But the man insisted: "Pastor, she's trying to poison me! I can even see the poison next to my plate. There's a part of my wife that you don't understand. I suggest you talk to her."

Well, later on that afternoon, the pastor came back and said to the man, "You know, I just spent three-and-a-half hours speaking with your wife. I have a suggestion for you."

"What is it?" the man asked.

"Just take the poison."

For some people, that fictitious story might be all too true! There are some people who are impossible in the sense that they are strong-willed, selfish, and have a hardened conscience; yet in their minds, their anger and selfishness is justified. They're willing to destroy others for their own selfish reasons. They have no desire to have a good conscience. Even worse, they may think that they already do!

Scripture tells us that in the last days, there will be teachers who are "liars whose consciences are seared" (1 Timothy 4:2). The King James Version says they are seared as "with a hot iron." The word that describes this is *cauterized*. That is, these people have feelings only for themselves, and have no sympathy or care for others. They have hardened consciences.

Paul also speaks about a *defiled* conscience. In fact we read that in some people "both their minds and their consciences are defiled" (Titus 1:15). They no longer acknowledge the difference between right and wrong, and they are blind to their manipulation, meanness, and self-serving love.

There is another passage in the New Testament that doesn't mention the word *conscience*, but it describes the kind of people I'm writing about. It begins, "But understand this, that in the last days there will come times of difficulty. For people will be lovers of self" (2 Timothy 3:1-2). Notice that Paul put *self-love* at the head of a long list of other sins. Then he finished his list: "lovers of money, proud, arrogant, abusive, disobedient to their parents, ungrateful, unholy, heartless, unappeasable, slanderous, without self-control, brutal, not loving good, treacherous, reckless, swollen with conceit, lovers of pleasure rather than lovers of God, having the appearance of godliness, but denying its power. Avoid such people" (verses 2-5).

What a description!

That word "unappeasable" jumped out at me, and later in this chapter, we'll learn that there are some people you can't reason with. Even if you are willing to meet them halfway (or beyond), they'll always demand more. Their ego needs are huge, but they think their outrageous demands are reasonable and right. They're incapable of showing sympathy for those they victimize. In today's world, they're called *narcissists*.

After writing that long list of sinful behaviors, Paul concluded

by saying, "Turn away from people like this. Avoid them if you can."
But of course sometimes you can't!

The Anatomy of a Narcissist

Let's tour the human heart. It'll be painful, because our subject
is *narcissism*, or self-love. As we saw above, it stands at the head of a
long list of sins, all of which flow from the sin of an inordinate, all-
consuming self-love. This is about people whose conscience is inac-
tive; or more accurately, their conscience is beyond feeling.

We have to admit that to some extent, all of us are narcissists. All
of us love ourselves and protect ourselves at all costs. But there is a
small percentage of people who carry self-love to such an extreme
that they're actually diagnosed as being narcissistic. This isn't just
a problem "out there" in the world; these people exist in churches
and are often found in positions of Christian leadership. Of course
they exist as attorneys, doctors, or factory workers as well. And
many a decent person has married a narcissist.

A point of clarification: In this chapter, I will always refer to
a narcissist with the pronoun *he*, but the population is equally
divided—there are as many female narcissists as there are male. I
use the pronoun *he* only as shorthand for saying he/she. So make
no mistake—there are female narcissists too.

The Origin of the Term

The word *narcissism* comes to us from Greek mythology. Narcissus was supposedly the son of a god; he was in love with himself
and was greatly admired by the people. The story goes that when
he looked into a pool of water, he saw his image and fell in love
with himself to such an extent that he lost his appetite. In another
version of the story, Narcissus, admiring himself, fell into the water
and drowned. Some say it was a suicide because he realized that the
beauty he saw was unattainable, beyond reach.

The bottom line: *Narcissism* can be defined as a fixation with oneself and one's appearance. In short, it's an inordinate and exaggerated self-love that, in the mind of the narcissist, is fully deserved. Their conscience is hard and unyielding, and they refuse to see themselves for what they are.

The Exaltation of Self-Love

Where did narcissism have its beginning? It was birthed when Satan said to Adam and Eve, "You shall be like God." And, that promise was at least partially fulfilled because man was free to live as he pleased.

Once man became his own god, he began to play the part. Just like the living and true God always does what is right and does as He pleases (see Psalm 115:3), the narcissist, in his own perverted way, thinks he's right about everything. And yes, he pretty well does whatever he pleases. He is, for the most part, unteachable because he truly believes he knows best, and that he possesses a perspective that no one else has. Or so he thinks.

We know that everything rightly exists for God and for His glory. As Scripture says, "Worthy are you, our Lord and God, to receive glory and honor and power, for you created all things, and by your will they existed and were created" (Revelation 4:11).

Just so, *the narcissist believes everything exists for him.*

Let me put it this way: A narcissist processes all information through two important questions:

How does this make *me* look?

How does this make *me* feel?

Feeling good about himself is incredibly important to a narcissist, and if someone else receives more recognition than he does, he becomes angry and resentful. He sees other people as existing to feed his ego, and if his ego is unfed, he becomes demanding, vengeful, and manipulative. He has a feeling that he should be honored, and if he doesn't receive what he perceives as being just and proper, he retaliates.

Narcissists have a sense of entitlement. They really believe that the world owes them, and when the world doesn't stand up and give them what they feel they deserve, they typically respond with a great deal of anger, disappointment, and depression. They are willing to go to extremes to get "justice" as they understand it, no matter how skewed in their favor it might be.

The narcissist is obsessed with his own glory, his own need for recognition. He may obsess about his appearance, his own exaggerated accomplishments, and his own expectation of being properly recognized. When he thinks of himself, he denies the ugly side of who he is and is careful to project a wonderful and kind image. But often he can't help himself and is quick to speak about his fantasies of success and overblown evaluations of his own abilities.

The narcissist has other "god-like" qualities as well. He is obsessed with control. Creating chaos or allowing it to develop is very important to a narcissist because it is a means of control; if he can keep everyone else off balance, he becomes the center of attention.

For example, the family has to keep wondering what Dad thinks, and he's not telling because he wants to be perceived as unpredictable and have the mystique of being inscrutable. At the same time, his opinions are very important to him and he expects others to have great respect for his ideas. He remains very difficult to please. The minute the children (or his wife) think they have figured out ways to please him, they discover they are wrong. Overnight, his expectations have changed. It's like kicking a field goal and, while the ball is still in the air, the goalposts get moved farther back so that you always fall short.

Narcissists are always critical. They belittle others to keep everyone beneath them, subservient to them, thus the faults of others must constantly be exposed while their own are excused, or even better, entirely denied.

Narcissists find it almost impossible to give a genuine compliment. They are loath to admit that someone else might have some good in them. And, in the mind of the narcissist, when someone else wins, he himself loses. He's resentful when someone else is honored because he thinks to himself, *That really should have been me.* After all, he is a god—at least, that's what the serpent told Adam and Eve in Eden.

The narcissist demands he must be the center of attention. When a narcissist walks into a room, he sees everyone else as the competition he must somehow diminish. He'll do this through criticism of others or by making his presence known and appreciated. When he talks, it's probably about himself and his accomplishments. He has to be the bride at every wedding, and the corpse at every funeral. It's all about him!

No wonder narcissists, the ultimate lovers of self, have a cauterized conscience. They're hypersensitive to their own feelings, but have no feelings for those they hurt. They find ways to manage their conscience, but are largely without sympathy and scrupulously self-absorbed. When they are mean to you, they think they are being much kinder than you deserve.

And if you divorce a narcissist? You'll soon discover that they have no interest in fairness or decency. Give them everything they ask for, and they'll want more. You'll come to realize that their real goal is not justice, but to vilify you, make you guilty of all their own failings, and, in short, destroy you.

I repeat: narcissists are hypersensitive about their own feelings, and have no sympathy for those around them.

Overblown Narcissism

Their Own Reality

What is a narcissist like? First, he has his own reality. To a narcissist, truth is dispensable if it gets in the way of his ego and what he wants to do. Therefore, truth is often twisted, if not ignored all together.

Just when you think that you've come to an agreement with a narcissist about some matter, you'll later learn that the truth has been skewed. What you remember and what he remembers are very different. You begin to say to yourself, *Am I crazy or is he crazy? I thought that we agreed on this.*

The narcissist creates his own reality and is convinced that his version of events is the real story. No matter what the issue, it is always other people who are at fault. And the truth is whatever he says it is.

We've learned that the conscience of a narcissist is cauterized, seared to the point that it is, for the most part, dead to all feeling. That is why they have no feelings for those they hurt. If they're abusers, they don't even hear the cry of their little boy saying, "No, Daddy, don't beat me."

They Feel Their Own Pain Intensely

Yet at the same time, narcissists feel their own pain very keenly. One of the best examples of narcissism in the Bible is Cain, whose story is recorded in Genesis 4:8-15. Cain killed his brother, Abel, and God said, "You are going to be a fugitive in the land."

Notice Cain's wounded reaction: "My punishment is greater than I can bear. Behold, you have driven me today away from the ground, and from your face I shall be hidden. I shall be a fugitive and a wanderer on the earth, and whoever finds me will kill me" (verses 13-14).

This was an Oscar-worthy performance of self-pity. Cain murdered his brother, and then he complained about being a fugitive and the possibility that someone might kill him! But God was gracious to Cain and put a mark on him so no one would harm him (verse 15).

A narcissist will stab you, leave you bleeding alongside of the road, and walk away feeling sorry for himself. Occasionally a narcissist will admit to something, but he'll minimize it. "Okay, I messed up. I had an affair. So I'm sorry. Let's move on!" There's no sense of the depth of the pain that he caused. There's no sense of the hurt because all that he cares about is, "Let's get this over with, because whatever I did isn't that big of a deal." The narcissist prefers to deny his evil actions, but when that's not possible, he minimizes them.

They Judge Others More Harshly Than Themselves

Narcissists see other people as entirely good or evil based on their own skewed standards. A narcissist will marry a woman and adore her. He'll tell her, "You're the greatest person in the world. I can't believe that I had the privilege of marrying you." *Yada, yada, yada.* But that comes to a stop as soon as she fails to meet his expectations, or supply what his ego needs (and she never could because a narcissist's ego needs are impossible to fulfill). From that point onward, instead of working through the difficulty, the narcissist demonizes his wife. She's the worst possible person. Everything that she does is wrong. As the saying goes, he will blow a boat out of the water and then wonder why it doesn't float.

As I explained, this is why spouses who go through divorce proceedings with a narcissist end up finding that no concession is enough. A husband with a narcissistic wife may say, "Okay, I'll give her the house and whatever else she wants just so we can have peace." But eventually he will discover that such concessions won't ever be enough because what she really wants is to destroy him.

While I don't want to belabor this point, it's important to recognize you simply can't reason with or please narcissists. That explains the word "unappeasable" in 2 Timothy 3:3. I had never really seen it before in this light.

Narcissists are *unappeasable!* They see the evil that is in them as belonging to you, so they lie, manipulate, and use their emotions to come up with their version of truth. They don't want or need facts. In their paranoia, they imagine that others are against them and after them.

You may ask them, "What are your facts?" And they'll reply with, "I just know it." What interesting people they are! They don't feel the "weight of sin" for the same reason that a dead body does not feel a hundred-pound weight.

Living with a Narcissist

"Avoid such people" Paul admonished in 2 Timothy 3:5. Great advice, but that's hard to do if you're married to a narcissist. Or if you have relatives that are narcissistic, or if you must work with a narcissist. Chances are you know such a person because about ten percent of the population is diagnosed as narcissistic[1] (although narcissists are difficult to diagnose, because they'd never go to a counselor to get help).

At a conference at which I was speaking, two couples approached me and each told me their children married narcissists and then divorced them. After one couple described their former daughter-in-law, I asked, "Didn't your son see any red flags in the relationship? Weren't there some signs that this young lady was narcissistic?"

The wife replied, "Yes, the first night he came home after meeting her, he said, 'I met this real cute girl, but she believes she's the center of the universe.'" That should have been his first clue!

Yes, she was cute. She was probably bubbly, very engaging, and lots of fun, as narcissists often are. In fact, they can be charmers, outwardly delightful and attractive, and can easily win you over. The people at the church might think he's the greatest guy in the world and envy the woman who's married to him. But at home it is an entirely different story, when the wife is expected to be the ego-suppliant to the narcissist.

One of my daughters is a counselor who often encounters narcissists. She wrote an unpublished paper describing them, and I summarize parts of it in the pages ahead. My goal is to arm you with some understanding of the way narcissists think and act so that you can perhaps help them *redemptively*. Perhaps their consciences can be resensitized.

Here's some practical advice for dealing with or getting along with narcissists, whether they are relatives or coworkers.

Listen to Their Story

Take a deep breath and remember that they too have a story. Have the patience to listen to them. They were probably abused or suffered a sense of abandonment when they were young. They may have been raised in an alcoholic home and may have developed a sense of self-protection that went on to become narcissism.

We should also remember that no matter how much evil narcissists do, there's more to them than the evil that they do. They are human beings created in God's image, and we need to minister to them and help them as much as we can.

Have Few Expectations

Lower your expectations. Don't be surprised when a narcissist suddenly turns from being charming to being cruel. A narcissist may seem happy and pleasant when friends are over for company, but as soon as their guests leave, their cheerfulness may turn into anger, control, and criticism without a reason.

When this happens, the narcissist's stunned spouse or friend may think, *Who in the world is this person? Isn't this the one we were just having fun with? How is it that he has turned so violently angry after the company left?* Remember that narcissists don't feel they have to *be* good, but they certainly feel they have to *look* good at all costs. So if you are dealing with a narcissist, lower your expectations. If they do seem to change for the better, don't expect it to last.

Become a Whole Person

Living with a narcissist is so difficult because the stress of trying to keep him happy and constantly feeding his ego will eventually take a toll. Meeting his impossible expectations can turn you into an automaton whose own spirit and personality have been crushed. But you need to be able to preserve yourself as a whole person in the midst of the struggle. One of the best ways to do this is to surround yourself with a community of people who'll encourage you and help you grow. I recommend finding a good church, and especially a small group of people who will pray with you and for you so that God will grant you the grace you need.

Don't Give in to Revenge

Here's a very important word for you if you are suffering under the constant browbeating of a narcissist: *When sinned against, do not sin in return*. In this we have the loving example of our Lord himself. The apostle Peter said,

> Christ...suffered for you, leaving you an example, so that you might follow in his steps. He committed no sin, neither was deceit found in his mouth. When he was reviled, he did not revile in return; when he suffered, he did not threaten, but continued entrusting himself to him who judges justly (1 Peter 2:21-23).

Take a lesson from David: When his enemy Saul threw a spear

at him, David fled; he did not pull the spear out of the wall and throw it back!

Remember, Narcissists Can Change

Let's ask an all-important question: Can a narcissist change? I believe they can, because I believe in God's power to bring change in a person's life. Nobody should be considered to be beyond the bounds of God's mercy and intervention through the gospel.

I also believe that narcissists occasionally have moments of clarity. One evening at a conference I preached on narcissism, and the next day a woman said to me, "You know, my husband is a narcissist."

She continued, "He was here last night, and our children looked at me as if to say, 'Guess who he's talking about.'"

Her husband, she said, was a Bible teacher (don't be surprised; narcissists often know the Bible, but they won't allow their knowledge to transform them). And he was always critical of the messages he heard from others because his standards were so high. So I asked what he thought of the message I gave. She said it was the first time, if she remembered correctly, that he drove home and said nothing about the message. Apparently a shaft of light entered his soul that night, and for a moment at least he saw himself for what he was.

Narcissists seldom see themselves as they really are, and for that matter, none of us do. We all hide, excuse ourselves, and show others our good side. But there are moments of clarity when God graciously pulls back the curtain of our self-justifying perspective so we see ourselves for who we really are. Without that awareness, change does not happen.

God's Invitation for Narcissists—and the Rest of Us

We all must be reminded that we live in the presence of a God who knows our insecurities and fears, a God who sees us so thoroughly that there is no reason for us to run and hide. Narcissists who insist on attention and the control of others should know that in the presence of God they can at last be truthful; God, our Father, can handle their anger, their jealousies, and their unacknowledged dishonesty.

That's why I believe Psalm 139 is so helpful toward bringing inner transformation. In the presence of a God who knows all about our thoughts and existence we can relax and admit to ourselves and to Him who we really are. So that we can better grasp the extent of God's knowledge of us and His willingness for us to come to Him, we will tour Psalm 139 with the hope that in the end, we will confess to whatever He exposes and receive the acceptance we all desire.

God Knows Us Exhaustively

David began by saying, "O LORD, you have searched me and known me!" (verse 1). God already knows everything about us; every bit of information—both actual and possible—is known to Him.

David continued, "You know when I sit down and when I rise up" (verse 2). How many times did you sit down and get up yesterday? I can't remember how many times I did so. But God knows the number, and He knows what happened fifty years ago as well as He knows what happened yesterday. His knowledge is accurate and complete.

"You discern my thoughts from afar" (verse 2). David was saying, "Before I even think a thought, You already know it." God knows how we deeply resent people who minimize us, who are more successful than we are at our own game, or who are more beautiful and more gifted than we are. God sees those thoughts.

God also sees when we hypocritically pretend that we love people and glad-hand them when we inwardly despise them. He also sees the images we watch on our computers and then erase. He sees all of these things. They are all entirely present to Him.

David went on: "Even before a word is on my tongue, behold, O LORD, you know it altogether" (verse 4). Before words are formed in our mind and we actually say them, God already knows them. Not only that, God knows the words we'd like to speak but dare not say publicly. He knows the words that are spoken only in our hearts.

If you are a narcissist, remember, God knows your fears. He knows how scared you are of being exposed in the presence of others you've lived to impress. He knows all the shame you're trying to hide. He knows how closed you are to the real truth about you. You come to church with your arms crossed, intending to be critical of everything because, after all, you can't let God get close to you and show you what you need to change.

But—and this is certainly true for all of us—God isn't thwarted by our closed minds or folded arms. He knows us exhaustively, so we may as well be honest when we come into His presence.

God Knows Us Eternally

Absolutely nothing is hidden from God. David continued in verses 9-12:

> If I take the wings of the morning and dwell in the uttermost parts of the sea, even there your hand shall lead me, and your right hand shall hold me. If I say, "Surely the darkness shall cover me, and light about me be night," even the darkness is not dark to you; the night is bright as the day, for darkness is as light with you.

By the way, most crime is committed at night because criminals use the cover of darkness to hide their deeds. But to God, everything we do is done as if in broad daylight. There's nothing we can hide.

David then became even more intimate in his praise of the knowledge of God: "You formed my inward parts; you knitted me together in my mother's womb" (verse 13). In effect he was saying, "You were there superintending the DNA that I'd eventually have, and the confluence of genes that would produce me."

It was God who made you as you are, and not like someone else. He was there supervising your fetal development. There were no mistakes, no time when God said, "Oops!" or "I didn't expect that." Has it ever dawned on you that nothing has ever dawned on God? Throughout all of eternity, He has known you. He already knows what lies ahead for you. He doesn't have to wait and see how it all turns out.

David then wrote, "My frame was not hidden from you, when I was being made in secret, intricately woven in the depths of the earth" (verse 15). When David was in his mother's womb, God was there. The psalmist continued, "Your eyes saw my unformed substance; in your book were written, every one of them, the days that were formed for me, when as yet there was none of them" (verse 16).

No wonder David then burst into praise: "How precious to me are your thoughts, O God! How vast is the sum of them!" (verse 17).

With every wave that laps upon a shoreline, the juxtaposition of the grains of sand changes. Because of the rapid rate at which waves keep coming upon the beach, the grains of sand are constantly being moved. Now think of it: God knows the longitude and the latitude of every grain of sand on the seashores of the world as they shift their position. Amazing!

God Shows Us What He Sees

Then David personalized his contemplations: "Search me, O God, and know my heart! Try me and know my thoughts!" (verse 23).

Wait a moment. Was David contradicting himself? He began the psalm with a statement of fact: "You have searched me and known me." But then he ended by saying, "Search me."

To clarify: If God has already searched him, why does he ask God to do it again? The answer is clear. David is saying, "Lord, I know that You know all about me, but now I'm asking You to *show me what You see*."

This is a prayer for all of us. When we are in God's presence, we can be totally honest because we're not telling Him anything that He doesn't already know. We can spill out our hearts and ask God to help us with self-discovery. We can say, "Show me as much of my true self as I am able to grasp; show me how my pride blocks Your grace. Show me my fears, my insecurities; show me my anger, vengeful spirit, and selfish heart. Take from me my cauterized conscience and replace it with a tender heart."

We want a conscience that is free of any offence; we want a sensitive conscience that can feel the pain of others. We don't want to be characterized as one who is "past feeling."

Secure in the knowledge that God knows us, we can admit who we are without fear of being rejected or thrown away. This, in turn, gives us the security to be honest with others. Our masks can fall to the ground because we have the assurance that we are loved and accepted by the God who knows our every fault yet still loves us.

No matter where we are on the continuum of narcissism, we can all join a Bible study and invite others to pray for us. We can give up the charade of our own perfection and rightness, and be honest before God and others.

Our Response to God's Truth

Jesus told a parable that illustrates the importance of honesty as a pathway to change. "Two men went up into the temple to pray, one a Pharisee and the other a tax collector. The Pharisee, standing by himself, prayed thus: 'God, I thank you that I am not like other men, extortioners, unjust, adulterers, or even like this tax collector. I fast twice a week; I give my tithes of all that I get'" (Luke 18:10-12).

In other words, the Pharisee was saying, "God, I have nothing to repent of. That tax collector over there does, but I don't. I stand in Your presence as one who is an example of prudence, discipline, and righteousness."

Jesus continued, "But the tax collector, standing far off, would not even lift up his eyes to heaven, but beat his breast, saying, 'God, be merciful to me, a sinner!' I tell you, this man went down to his house justified, rather than the other" (verses 13-14).

Note how the tax collector prayed, "God be propitious, be satisfied, and grant me the grace of Your forgiveness." He was praying in faith, looking ahead to God's promise of a Redeemer who would satisfy the demands of His holiness—which is exactly why Jesus died on the cross. He died as a sacrifice so that all who believe on Him may be saved.

Let us return for a moment to the list of sins that we referenced at the beginning of this chapter. Paul ended by saying of such people that they "[have] the appearance of godliness, but [deny] its power" (2 Timothy 3:5). They profess to know God, but they know nothing of His power because they have never been transformed by Him.

Jesus was teaching us that *it's easier for us to repent of our sins than it is to repent of our self-righteousness!* If the narcissist doesn't see his need to repent of anything, there's little hope of changing his behavior. It's not enough for him to see himself as guilty of individual sins; he needs to realize he is a hardened sinner who needs to be broken by God. Repentance should be more than a momentary experience for us; it should lead to a lifelong and complete dependence on God.

There is hope for the broken sinner who calls on God in

desperation because he has realized his sinfulness. But there is no hope for the self-righteous who admit that they have messed up but aren't as bad as others. Self-righteousness is the greatest enemy of emotional and spiritual healing. It, more than any other sin, stands in the way of fulfilling relationships.

Grace cannot enter closed doors.

A Passage to Ponder:

God opposes the proud, but gives grace to the humble. Submit yourselves therefore to God. Resist the devil, and he will flee from you. Cleanse your hands, you sinners, and purify your hearts, you double minded...Humble yourselves before the Lord, and he will exalt you (James 4:6-8, 10).

Probing Questions to Consider:

Are you willing to take the time to have God reveal to you the needs of your inner heart? What changes do you sense need to be made with regard to your attitudes? What action steps can you start taking now to bring about those changes?

9

Forever Forgiven

Bring your sins, and He will bear them away into the
wilderness of forgetfulness, and you
will never see them again.

D.L. Moody

The great Reformer Martin Luther struggled mightily with his conscience. In fact, that is why he became a monk. He was desperate to quiet his tormented soul. He experienced an overwhelming sense of guilt and despair over his failures.

As a monk, he renounced self-will, slept on a floor without a blanket, and engaged in other acts of self-sacrifice in an attempt to mortify the flesh. He carried out these disciplines rigorously—including the confession of all his sins. Sometimes he would spend hours in confession, all in an effort to make sure no sin, no matter how seemingly trivial, went unconfessed. Yet still his conscience tormented him.

It was through the reading of Scripture that Luther eventually came to realize he was doing it all wrong. He had thought that if he fulfilled all the right requirements—including a complete confession of all his sins—somehow he would become right before God. But Romans 1:17 caught his attention: "The righteous shall live by faith." As he continued reading through Romans, he realized that righteousness is a gift that God *gives* to sinners. As Romans 4:3 says, "Abraham believed God, and it was counted to him as righteousness."

Day and night, Luther pondered the connection between "The righteous shall live by faith" and the fact that righteousness had been given to Abraham. He said that when he realized that righteousness is a gift, it was as if he had walked through the gates of Paradise. It didn't matter how high God's standard was (which is absolute, perfect righteousness). As long as Jesus Himself kept that standard and did so on behalf of Luther, he was free. He was forgiven. He was righteous before God.

As 2 Corinthians 5:21 says, God "made him to be sin who knew no sin, so that in him we might become the righteousness of God." Follow carefully: Jesus got what He didn't deserve (our sin) so that we could get what we didn't deserve (His righteousness). This was the great exchange. One hymn writer described it this way:

Well might the sun in darkness hide
And shut his glories in,
When Christ, the great Maker died,
For man the creature's sin.[1]

God Has Taken Care of It All

Let us turn now to Romans 8, one of the greatest chapters in the entire Bible. If the Bible were a ring with many different gemstones in it, the middle stone—that is, the point of the diamond—would be the book of Romans. And then, of course, the center point of that would be Romans chapter 8.

The apostle Paul opened the chapter with this great declaration: "There is therefore now no condemnation for those who are in Christ Jesus." And he closed it with this incredible assurance:

Who shall bring any charge against God's elect? It is God who justifies. Who is to condemn? Christ Jesus is the one who died—more than that, who was raised—who is at the right hand of God, who indeed is interceding for us. Who shall separate us from the love of Christ? Shall tribulation, or distress, or persecution, or famine, or nakedness, or danger, or sword?...No, in all these things we are more than conquerors through him who loved us. For I am sure that neither death nor life, nor angels nor rulers, nor things present nor things to come, nor powers, nor height nor depth, nor anything else in all creation, will be able to separate us from the love of God in Christ Jesus our Lord (verses 33-39).

Take a closer look at the question Paul asked in verse 33: "Who shall bring any charge against God's elect?" Well, perhaps there are some wrongdoings for which you can be charged—by your spouse, by your coworkers, by the police. Or perhaps your conscience can bring a charge against you. It reminds you of something you did in the past, and as a result, you feel guilt. That was the challenge Luther faced.

When it comes to guilt, our tendency is to wallow in it. And Satan is all too glad to help us along. The Bible says that he accuses the saints day and night. It's a full-time job for him. He accuses us not just with words, but with our feelings. So we feel condemned, inferior, unable to please God. We may even feel self-hatred because we just can't seem to overcome certain temptations once and for all.

No matter what the source of the charges, however, we must remember this: "It is God who justifies" (verse 33). That is, He has a different verdict. If we have received the righteousness offered to us by Christ's death on the cross, and we've received it by faith, then we have been forgiven. Yes, God has forgiven us, and He has done much more than that.

In Romans 8, Paul makes it clear that we are not only forgiven, but God has legally declared us to be as righteous as He Himself is. Luther understood that nobody gets to heaven unless he's as perfect as God. And that's correct. There is simply no way we can achieve that kind of righteousness. Unless, of course, God gives it to us.

The biblical term for what God has done is *justification*. It's a legal term by which God says, "In my sight, I pronounce you perfect, forgiven, forever."

Perhaps you have already heard this illustration before, but it so perfectly depicts what we're talking about here that I want to share it. Suppose you were caught speeding on the highway. You appear in court, and it's clear that you're guilty. You must be punished. That's when the judge, who is kindhearted, leaves the bench, takes off his robe, stands beside you, pulls out his wallet, and pays the fine himself. Then he goes back to the bench and says, "You are acquitted. Your debt has been paid in full. So far as the law is concerned, you are under no condemnation because I paid the debt for you."

That's what justification by faith means. Jesus Christ, through His death on the cross, paid your debt. Because of your sin, you faced eternal condemnation, eternal separation from God. But Christ took that punishment upon Himself and in exchange, gave you His righteousness.

Some people say, "So justification is *just as if I'd never sinned*." Yes, it's that, but it's much more than that. It's not only as if you'd never sinned, but it's as if you had lived a life of perfect and complete obedience before God. We are saved entirely on the basis of God's righteousness being gifted to us.

What It Means to Be Justified by God

What I'd like to do in the rest of this chapter is to unpack this idea of justification. Once you grasp how big a deal justification is, you'll probably find these truths crossing your mind just about every day for the rest of your life. Very seldom does a day go by during which I myself am not reminded about these great truths from Scripture. These truths will help you to feel an incredible sense of deliverance from guilt and a troubled conscience.

Below are five short words or phrases that help to summarize what justification is all about.

1. Free Gift

Obviously the righteousness of God, which is credited to us, has to be given to us by God as a free gift. We cannot achieve it on our own. We cannot earn it. We cannot add to it. In the same way that a billion bananas will never produce an orange, all the human righteousness in the world can never attain to the righteousness of God. If we're going to become righteous, it has to be given to us by God. Our works can contribute absolutely nothing to it.

Do you realize what that means? As sinners, we all stand condemned before God. We are all unrighteous. Even if you've never committed murder or carried out some other seriously grievous behavior, you are still unrighteous—just as the worst sinner is unrighteous.

So when it comes to forgiving someone, God does not find it harder to forgive and accept a greater sinner than a lesser one. His forgiveness takes you from your wholly unrighteous state—no matter how "little" or "great" your sin—and credits His perfect righteousness to you. Because of what Christ did on the cross, you go from condemned to accepted. That's equally true for all who put their faith in Christ, no matter what their past.

Someone in prison wrote to me and said he had sexually assaulted four women and destroyed their lives. His question was, "Can I be forgiven?" Well, because what he did was so horribly wrong, our first reaction would probably be, "No, just go to hell where you belong." But then we have to remember that hell is where we belong too. As Romans 3:10-11 says, "None is righteous, no, not one...no one seeks for God."

To return to an illustration I mentioned earlier in this book, I wrote to him and I basically said this: "Imagine there are two trails.

One trail is well-traveled. It is smooth, and it has beautiful flowers along the path. The other trail is a mess. It is filled with deep ruts. It is ugly and difficult to take.

"Imagine a storm comes along and drops 18 inches of snow. You can't tell the difference between the two trails because both of them have been covered by the snow."

"Come now, let us reason together, says the LORD: though your sins are like scarlet, they shall be as white as snow; though they are red like crimson, they shall become like wool" (Isaiah 1:18). And I told this prisoner, "Yes, the righteousness of Christ can cover your sins just like it covered mine." That is the good news of the gospel: God's forgiveness is given freely to those who believe. It is a free gift. No matter how much we might attempt to please God through our own good works, the ledger will never end up in our favor. Without God's gift, we are headed to judgment. But because Jesus paid the penalty for our sins, He can give us the righteousness of God.

2. Complete

If you've struggled with past sins and doubted God's forgiveness, what I'm about to share here could be a means of deliverance for you. When you receive Jesus as your Savior, your sins are legally forgiven—past, present and future. That is, you've been forgiven *completely*. It has to be that way, and that's exactly what the Bible teaches. How many of your sins were future when Jesus Christ died? All of them, because you were not on the scene 2000 years ago when Jesus died. When He went to the cross, He died for sins not yet committed. He anticipated what you would do, and covered those sins with His offering on the cross. Hebrews 10:14 says, "For by a single offering he has perfected for all time those who are being sanctified." Did you catch that phrase "perfected for all time"? The word "perfected" here refers to something that has been accomplished and is finished. It's *completed*.

We find this affirmed in Colossians 2:13-14 as well:

> You, who were dead in your trespasses and the uncircumcision of your flesh, God made alive together with him, having forgiven us all our trespasses, by canceling the record of debt that stood against us with its legal demands. This he set aside, nailing it to the cross.

Back in those days, when a person was crucified, the crime he had committed was posted in an inscription above him. In Jesus' case, Pilate had written, "This is the King of the Jews" (Luke 23:38). That was His crime—declaring Himself to be the Messiah. It was nailed to the cross.

All of your sins, figuratively speaking, were nailed to the cross. And God said, "I'm going to take care of all those sins by having Jesus pay the penalty for them." Imagine how Luther felt when he realized that all his sins no longer belonged to him—they belonged to Jesus. Again, as 2 Corinthians 5:21 says, "He made him to be sin who knew no sin, so that in him we might become the righteousness of God."

If all salvation did was take care of our past sins, then you'd never have any assurance that you are truly right with God because who knows what will happen tomorrow, or the next day? You'd have to confess any new sins you commit.

But Scripture says your justification is complete. It's a finished work. You are free from the never-ending treadmill of good works done in the hopes of pleasing God. When you received Christ as your Savior, your decision affected not just your past sins, but your eternity.

That brings up a question: Do we as Christians still confess our sins as life goes on? Yes! Having received the good news of the gospel, having all of our sins taken care of legally from now until all the way to heaven's door and beyond, yes, we do. It's a discipline that God puts us through so that we might be able to walk in continuous fellowship with Him. Our salvation is forever secure—all our sins have been forgiven. That's our *position* before God. But in *practice*, we still sin from day to day. And that disrupts our relationship with God. As I've already emphasized earlier, by confessing what we've done, we should at the same time affirm what is true about our position: that we have been declared righteous in God's eyes. Indeed, we can be out of fellowship with God, but our legal standing remains firm.

3. Guarantee

When you receive the righteousness of Jesus Christ and you accept Him as your Savior, that means that your destination is guaranteed for all eternity. As we saw earlier, Paul asked in Romans 8:35, "Who shall separate us from the love of Christ? Shall tribulation, or distress, or persecution, or famine, or nakedness, or danger, or sword?" And the resounding answer in the verses that follow is that nothing will separate us—*nothing*!

Jesus said of His sheep, "They will never perish, and no one will snatch them out of my hand. My Father, who has given them to me, is greater than all, and no one is able to snatch them out of the Father's hand" (John 10:28-29).

As a believer, your destination is secure. That's why, in Ephesians 2, Paul wrote that God "made us alive together with Christ—by grace you have been saved—and *raised us up with him in the heavenly places in Christ Jesus*" (verses 5-6, emphasis added). Note that Paul wrote "raised up" in the past tense. In Jesus, we are already seated in heavenly places—it's a done deal. We can have complete assurance that when we die, we *will* go to heaven.

4. Personal Assurance

Even after you are acquitted by God, you may still struggle with feelings of guilt. For example, consider the example I gave earlier of the driver who was caught speeding. Though it was the driver who had violated the law and deserved to be punished, the judge decided to pay the penalty himself—even though he had done no wrong.

Now, it's possible the driver might leave the courtroom and say to himself, "I know I was guilty of going beyond the speed limit. Even though the judge has forgiven me, I still feel guilty."

If that's how you feel about something in your past, then what you need to do is educate your conscience, because your conscience is lying to you. It is telling you that you are guilty of something that God has acquitted you for. Now, it's possible that, from a human perspective, you'll have to live out the consequences of wrongdoing (such as paying the fine for a speeding ticket). That's to be expected. But before God, the slate is entirely clean. You've been forgiven. So if you're still feeling guilty, you need to retrain your conscience. Don't trust your feelings, for they will scream lies to you in an attempt to drag you down.

For example, some time ago I was on my way to a speaking engagement in a church in Michigan. For some reason or other, I was very angry. As I parked the car some 15 minutes before I was to speak, I felt guilty. I felt like a failure. I felt the weight of sin upon me. And I began to wonder: Could I go into the pulpit feeling so angry and yet preach and talk about the great beauties of the gospel?

I was alone in the car, and I spoke out loud to the devil and said, "Be gone, Satan, for it is written, 'Who shall bring any charge against God's elect? It is God who justifies. Who is to condemn? Christ Jesus is the one who died—more than that, who was raised—who is at the right hand of God, who indeed is interceding for us'" (Romans 8:33-34). And within a matter of minutes, my conscience was brought in line with the truth of Scripture, and I was able to preach a message similar to what I'm sharing in this chapter. A missionary who was present came up to me afterward and said, "If I had heard this message twenty years ago, I would have been delivered from all the guilt and struggles that I've experienced on the mission field during those years."

So yes, there are times when we need to educate our conscience so that it's in accordance with the Word of God. At the same time, however, you don't want to stifle your conscience. You don't want to block it out. But when you're feeling guilt for that which has been forgiven, you need to say, "Conscience, you perform an important function in my life, but right now you are lying to me. There is no condemnation for those who are in Christ Jesus." As a believer, you stand righteous before God because of the work of Jesus Christ!

5. Elect

Going back to Romans 8, Paul wrote, "Who shall bring any charge against God's elect?" (verse 33). Who are the "elect"? They are the ones God marked out from before the foundation of the world to become saved. He would overcome their darkness and unbelief and bring them to saving faith in Jesus.

You might say, "I don't like that at all. What if I want to become saved and I'm not among the ones God chose?" That's why it's important to remember what Jesus said in John 6:37: "All that the Father gives me will come to me, and whoever comes to me I will never cast out." If the Spirit is working in your heart and you come to Jesus, then you can know that you are among the elect.

Here's an illustration I've given often to explain justification. Some years ago, I was talking with a man who eventually died of AIDS. His life was a mess before he came to saving faith in Jesus Christ. As we were talking, I said to him, "Roger, imagine there are two books. One is titled *The Life and Times of Roger*. You open it up, and it's filled with sordid details about all kinds of sins and betrayal. The other book is titled *The Life and Times of Jesus Christ*.

You open it up, and there's nothing but beauty, perfection, meeting God's standards in everything. It's a beautiful book!

"When you came to saving faith in Christ, God said, in effect, 'I'm going to tear out all the pages inside your book, Roger, and insert the pages from My book inside your covers.' So now when you open *The Life and Times of Roger,* you'll see nothing but beauty and holiness. The book is so beautiful that even God adores it."

That is the gospel. That is what justification does. Jesus takes away your sin and, in exchange, credits God's righteousness to you.

I love these words from a hymn:

> The terror of law and of God
>
> With me can have nothing to do.
>
> My Savior's obedience and blood
>
> Hide all of my sins from view.
>
> My name on the palm of His hands
>
> Eternity will not erase.
>
> Impressed on His heart it remain,
>
> In marks of indelible grace.[2]

If you are expecting to please God through your good works, then you'll never have the assurance of eternal life. You'll never know if you've finally become good enough. Besides, as Scripture says, it's impossible for you to get to heaven by your own efforts.

Only when you trust that Christ has taken care of all that for you will you have assurance. His perfect sacrifice is for all time— for all eternity. Nothing will ever change that. Nothing can separate you from Him.

His forgiveness is forever.

And you have been made righteous before God—forever.

A Passage to Ponder:

What then shall we say to these things? If God is for us, who can be against us? He who did not spare his own Son but gave him up for us all, how will he not also with him graciously give us all things? Who shall bring any charge against God's elect? It is God who justifies. Who is to condemn? Christ Jesus is the one who died—more than that, who was raised—who is at the right hand of God, who indeed is interceding for us (Romans 8:31-34).

Probing Questions to Consider:

Are there any past sins you've already confessed to the Lord that you've had great difficulty letting go of? Do you truly believe God's grace has covered those sins, and that they have been forgiven? Read both Romans 8:1 and 1 John 1:9. What assurances can you claim from these passages? Do you agree God has forgiven your sins once and for all?

In this chapter we looked at five words or phrases that help to summarize what justification is all about:

1. Free gift
2. Complete
3. Guarantee
4. Personal assurance
5. Elect

Which of these words or phrases spoke most to your heart, and why?

10

When Sorry Isn't Enough

The reason why many are still troubled, still seeking, still making little forward progress is because they haven't yet come to the end of themselves. We're still trying to give orders, and interfering with God's work within us.

A. W. TOZER

When is confession to God not enough? When is it necessary for us to confess our wrongdoings to others so that we can experience the emotional freedom that a clear conscience brings? And, what do we do when saying sorry isn't enough?

The title for this chapter is taken from the book *When Sorry Isn't Enough*, written by my good friend Gary Chapman and co-author Jennifer Thomas.[1] I'll begin by presenting some basic principles for clearing one's conscience, and then I will summarize some thoughts from Chapman's excellent book. Let me warn you up front that I won't be able to answer all the questions that can arise in sticky situations regarding attempts at reconciliation. But I hope to give guidance that can be applied as we seek God's wisdom.

As we look at both principles and examples about rectifying broken relationships, we need to tread carefully, asking God to show us the way. Every situation is different, every difference of opinion has its own context, and every emotional injury has its own timetable for healing.

There are some people for whom repentance comes too easily;

they admit to their sins to be sure, but there is no heartfelt recognition of wrong. Those they have sinned against feel deep pain in their hearts, but the offender is satisfied with a cursory admission of wrongdoing. We've already learned that there are some people who keenly feel the hurt done to them yet are unable to enter into the pain of those whom they have wronged.

Perhaps the most common barrier to reconciliation is adultery, an offense that ruptures the marriage bond. A man (or a woman), consistently lies about where he was and who he is with; he manipulates his wife with guilt, diminishing her value and otherwise verbally abusing her. And then finally, when he can't deny the evidence, he says, "Okay, I messed up. I'm sorry!"

But his wife knows that sorry isn't enough. If she's wise she'll know that a simple confession isn't an adequate basis for true reconciliation to take place. A confession alone won't wipe the slate clean. That's because *when sin is taken superficially, it is dealt with superficially.*

On one level, it's true to say that we can be reconciled to others through confession. But if we minimize our transgressions, if we don't feel the pain of those we've wronged; if we're too quick to pronounce ourselves cured, if we chide those around us for not quickly forgetting what we've done, then our attempt at reconciliation is probably all too superficial.

As said in an earlier chapter, darkness can become a refuge, a safe place to retreat to when we fear exposure. Left to ourselves, we hate the light of the truth about ourselves—we might fear it more than sickness or even death. As we've learned, the self that we present to others in our social relationships is often quite different from the self that actually exists. Exposure surfaces humiliation, shame, and the erosion of trust. Once a person has been offended and hurt, the process of reconciliation can become a process with an uncertain ending.

There was woman who had seen many counselors yet couldn't

cope with her intense depression. Despite hours of counsel, she had withheld one important bit of information from them. As a teenage girl, she had given birth to a baby and had the infant killed to avoid the stigma that comes from public awareness of an illicit sexual affair. She married and had children, but chose to deaden her conscience by assuring herself that God had forgiven her, and that her husband didn't need to know about her past. But—and this is important—her husband was feeling the effects of her suppressed sin every day: her anger, her depression, her criticism—all because she had determined that this one blot on her life could never be exposed.

But finally, unable to live with herself any longer, she confessed her dark secret—first to her pastor, then to her husband. Thankfully, he was willing to forgive her. They went for counseling, and today are emotionally in tune with one another. And the unseen but powerful barrier that she had erected in their relationship is vanishing.

We can't pretend that all that we need is God's forgiveness if there are unresolved issues between us and others. Confession to God is relatively easy; after all, He knows all about us, which puts us at greater ease about being honest with Him. But reconciling with others is quite another story. And that is what this chapter is about.

Jesus taught us to not ignore the importance of one-on-one reconciliation. "If you are offering your gift at the altar and there remember that your brother has something against you, leave your gift there before the altar and go. First be reconciled to your brother, and then come and offer your gift" (Matthew 5:23-24). Jesus was saying, "When you come to God with an offering, if you remember that you are out of sorts with a fellow believer, leave your sacrifice there at the altar and go and be reconciled to the other person. Then come and offer your sacrifice to God."

According to Jesus, *reconciliation precedes worship*. So before you come to church to worship, be sure that you are reconciled to others. Then come to church and sing the praises of God and present your offerings. The matter that separates you from someone else might also be a barrier between you and God. True, there are some people with whom we cannot reconcile, but we must do all we can to rectify broken relationships.

The purpose of this chapter is to bring us to the point where we can say, with the apostle Paul, "I always take pains to have a clear conscience toward both God and man" (Acts 24:16). And if reconciliation fails, I can at least rest in peace knowing it has been attempted.

Principles of Reconciliation

In Matthew 18, Jesus said, "If your brother sins against you, go and tell him his fault, between you and him alone. If he listens to you, you have gained your brother. But if he does not listen, take one or two others along with you, that every charge may be established by the evidence of two or three witnesses" (verses 15-16).

Applying these principles is often messy. But let's think through what our obligations are, remembering that our goal is that God be glorified and our conscience cleared. We begin with some basic, commonsense principles.

Sins of the Heart Confessed to God Alone

The first principle is that sins of the heart should be confessed to God alone. Wouldn't the world be a terrible place if we all said what we thought of one another all the time? Can you imagine the fiasco? "Joe, do you know what I thought about you last Wednesday? Let me just tell you what came to mind." And soon Joe would tell you what he thought about you in even greater detail than your confession about him. Thank the Lord that the blood of Jesus

Christ covers all sin, and that there are many sins that do not need to be confessed to others if they have not resulted in actions that have erected an emotional barrier between us and someone else.

But let's be clear. If you have a poisoned attitude toward someone, you can't just say, "Well, it's only in my thoughts." If that attitude affected your relationship, you have to confess it because it was more than just a thought. You may not think that your anger against someone has to be confessed, but if that person has felt the effects of that anger, or has been the recipient of your attitude and actions, you need reconciliation through personal one-on-one confession. Certainly the secret of a good marriage is two people who are able to ask for forgiveness and receive it in the common and often difficult experiences of life. But there are many private thoughts that don't need to see the light of day.

Sins of Deception Must Be Confessed

Confession to God is not enough when there are matters of cheating or deception that we have hidden deep within us. Often, after years of rationalizing, a person will finally confront past issues that should have been addressed back when they happened. Recently I received an email from a student of mine who admitted to cheating in a class I taught thirty-six years ago. She had used the research of another student to write her term paper. She confessed her sin to God and knew that He had forgiven her, but she did not experience total restoration. So she did what many people do—she kept pushing the matter deep into her heart. She would forget about it for a time, but then it would resurface.

She wrote, "While reading the book *Gripped by the Greatness of God* (James MacDonald), I was brought up short and knew I could not go one more day without taking care of this matter once and for all. [MacDonald] said that 'it's your sin that keeps you from the incredible grace and greatness of God. Sin distances your heart from the Lord's abundant provision for you' (page 120). This hit me over the head. It seems no matter how hard I have tried to know the fullness of God in my life recently, I have continued to struggle. It was this chapter that brought me up short. My disobedience to the prompting of the Holy Spirit to swallow my pride and send you this letter was staring me right in the face. I could not go on today until I took care of this matter."

Of course I forgave her, but I could not help but think of the many people who keep such secrets locked in their hearts. God has forgiven them, but their conscience keeps telling them that everything is "not quite right." If that is true about cheating on a term paper thirty-six years ago, it certainly applies to the more serious deceptions often faced in marriage.

Addictions that rupture relationships—whether they be overt or secret—should be confessed. That includes drugs, pornography, theft, and the like. These kinds of private sins spill over into public relationships both within the family and beyond it. Unconquered hidden sins often affect all whom we meet; they affect our attitudes, fuel resentment, and rob us of joy. Addictions set up unseen barriers that interfere with interpersonal intimacy and trust.

Of course all sin is deceitful, but because sexual sins are so prevalent, I want to address them because they often occur within a marriage. In the opening pages of this book I told about a man who had fathered a child in his college days. This child is growing up in another city, and neither the man's wife nor his children know about this boy. This man wants to worship God. Rationalize it as he might, the reality is that he can't really have clarity in his relationship with his wife, and therefore can't have a clear conscience before God, unless that secret is revealed and forgiven.

He needs to carefully think through when and how the matter is approached; but yes, he won't find joy in God until that issue is confessed to his wife, and eventually, to his children. His wife will likely have to be counseled on the matter of forgiveness, but if their marriage is strong, it should survive the shock. And it's better that his wife hear about this from her husband rather than from his son, who someday might just show up on their doorstep and say, "Hi...you are my Dad." And confession may help his wife understand other matters in their relationship as well.

Here's another true story (using fictitious names): Fred marries Ann, who carries on an affair during the early years of their marriage. She's convicted about her behavior, and breaks off the affair. Years later, she tells her past lover, Peter, that she's going to tell her husband about her deceitful tryst. When her husband, Fred, hears about her affair with Peter, he becomes very angry because he and Peter had been friends. Peter is also angry—*very* angry—that Ann exposed him. He feels doubly guilty for having betrayed both his own wife and his friend, Fred.

Did Ann do the right thing? Some counselors would say no because the affair was in the past. But can Ann and her husband have an open, honest relationship with each other? I doubt it, and by the way, nor can Peter have a mutually satisfying relationship with his wife as long as his affair remains a secret. He is angry at Ann, but sin always has unintended consequences, and now he will have to deal with matters in his own marriage.

Ann wanted to have a clear conscience, which is why she confessed. Interestingly enough, when Ann confessed to Fred, it turned out that he also had something to confess that he had been hiding from her. Although his sin was not the same kind as hers, the relationship needed rebuilding from both sides of the marriage bond. They survived the reconciliation process, and they are enjoying a deep, caring, and trusting relationship today.

Here is a letter written by a woman who reconciled after committing adultery:

> I committed adultery. I thought maybe the devil was convicting me because I had confessed this sin many times to the Lord and had received forgiveness. After all,

I reasoned that God wouldn't want me to hurt my husband. I was determined to keep it to myself and deal with it when I died. I wrestled with the decision...then...I knew I could ignore it no longer.

The news of my affair was a lot for [my husband] to endure, but when he heard it, he embraced me with love and compassion. I was, and still am, overcome with gratitude and am thankful that God loves me and so does my husband. The days since have been challenging; we've spent a great deal of time together talking and praying.

Difficult though it has been, I'm thankful God did not let me die in that sinful state. God again has proven His love to me. I'm a living witness of His amazing grace, His tender mercy, and loving kindness.

Have a Third Party at the Confession

When appropriate, others should be present during the reconciliation process. Jesus said in Matthew 18:16 that if you go to your brother and he refuses to be reconciled, go back and take one or two other people with you as witnesses. But when you desire a clear conscience and want to pursue reconciliation, I believe that it's wise right from the beginning to have someone else be present during this time of confession. Yes, it's difficult to shed one's pride and invite a pastor or counselor into the process, but it may help to facilitate the process.

As a pastor, I've helped offer counsel in such situations. For example, one woman asked me to be present when she had to confess to her husband that their third child was not his. Either she had to tell him or suffer a nervous breakdown; she couldn't handle the guilt and deception. Her husband was not just shocked, but stunned. As they talked, many things he had observed but didn't understand began to make sense. Now he better understood why his third child "didn't seem to fit" with the family. And although the confession brought anger, betrayal, and bitterness to the surface, it also explained many things about their own relationship as a couple. It was a difficult encounter, and without me or some other counselor present, the reconciliation process just might have gotten out of hand.

There is no doubt in my mind that this wife did what she had to do. The human psyche can only manage so much guilt. There's a lesson here: If we clear our side of the ledger, we can't ultimately be held responsible for the response of the other party. I prayed that this husband would find the grace in his heart to forgive his wife and rebuild his marriage, and even to trust God that He would bless that third child. Unfortunately, the couple ended up getting a divorce.

You may ask, "Are there times when such matters shouldn't be confessed?" The answer is *yes*. For example, if the relationship is already so frayed and tenuous, so weak and falling apart, then perhaps it's best to confess it to someone else—to a pastor or a counselor, because relationships that are already strained might find the confession only hastens the breaking point.

Timing is important. Think of the man who, just before he died, confessed to his wife, "Fifteen years ago I had an affair, and now that I'm dying, I need to get it off my chest so I can have a clear conscience when I enter into eternity." When I heard about what had happened, I was angry.

I would have told the dying man, "Well, thank you very much! How wonderful of you to try to clear your conscience right before you die by dumping this information on your wife, who has to process it alone for the rest of her life." His deathbed confession ended up leaving his wife distraught for years to come. Obviously he should have confessed his sin when it happened so the two of them could have worked through the betrayal together. Having waited as long as he did, this dying man would have done better to confide in a pastor, counselor, or some trusted friend. All that to say, we should not die with secrets.

I would like to think that Christian marriages have the relational strength to weather practically any storm. But reconciliation is a stool with three legs. There must be *respect, trust,* and *forgiveness* that takes into account the depth of the betrayal. Forgiveness must be both requested and granted. Of course, trust, once shattered, takes time to rebuild.

The confession should be as broad as the offense. It's not necessary for everyone to know about your failure, but the people who have been affected by the hurt need to know. In fact, there are times when, in the case of an elder or other church leader, confession should be made to the whole church if his sin has affected the congregation.

Ask: Who has my betrayal affected? Then pray that God will give you wisdom to proceed with the reconciliation process.

Five Ways to Say You're Sorry

Now let's turn to some thoughts from Gary Chapman and Jennifer Thomas's book *When Sorry Isn't Enough.* I want to mention five different ways that you can say you're sorry—and sometimes, all five ways are necessary to ask for complete forgiveness.

Expressing Regret

Sometimes "I'm sorry" is all that is needed, especially in minor matters. "I'm sorry that I spilled some coffee on your coat." I suspect every husband has had to say, "I'm sorry that I forgot to take out the garbage." A wife may say, "I'm sorry that I didn't get home on time to help with dinner."

The key here is to specifically identify what you are sorry for.

And then not blame the other person for what you did wrong! And, furthermore, the person who is receiving the apology should be willing to say, "I accept your apology and forgive you." In everyday scenarios like the ones described above that should take care of the breach in the relationship.

But sometimes just saying "I'm sorry" isn't enough. I know of one husband who took the couple's savings and invested the money in a get-rich-quick scheme on the Internet, and lost all of their retirement funds. For him to say, "I'm sorry—I messed up! Let's just move on and pretend that this was no big deal" simply won't do.

That's because what he did *was* a big deal! This was no time for a superficial "Oh, I'm sorry" response. That couple was sure to feel the effects of his foolishness well into their retirement years. The husband asking for forgiveness had to consider not only how his sin would affect him, but his wife as well. When we wrong others, we must face the hurt and pain we've caused by our betrayal.

Accept Responsibility

A second-level of confession is to say, "I was wrong. I accept responsibility. This was no minor matter." And when you say, "I was wrong," you do not add, "But look at what *you* did." You must take your responsibility so seriously that even if you think you're only thirty percent at fault, you must look at that thirty percent as if it were one hundred percent! And if the other person doesn't take any responsibility for their part in the issue, that's between them and God.

Unfortunately, there are some people you just can't reconcile with. They're so toxic and so skewed, and their reality is so different from yours, that when you admit wrong to them, they might go so far as to expect you to confess to something you *didn't* do. And if they will not own up to their own wrongdoings, you may have to accept that there can be no true reconciliation. At best you might treat one another politely, but there will be no unity of mind and heart.

But—and this is important—when we hurt someone, that person will want to make sure we realize the extent of the pain we caused. That's why saying "I'm sorry" isn't enough. For example, if you've ruined your marriage, your confession must be deeply genuine and heartfelt. In such situations, you should be willing to articulate the pain you've caused: "I know that my actions did this, this, and this to you." The other person needs to know that you understand the hurt you've inflicted.

You need to own up to your failure, and the other person needs to know that you understand the consequences of your actions. You need to say, "I know what I did was wrong. I know I've hurt you deeply. I own up to my mistakes, failures, and sins. Could you find it in your heart to forgive me?"

Accepting responsibility for your failures will go a long way toward restoring your relationship.

Seek to Make Things Right

The third suggestion offered by the authors of *When Sorry Isn't Enough* is that we demonstrate our sorrow by asking how we can make things right. There are some things you can't make right, but there are other things that you can—for example, through restitution. We see this in Luke 19:1-10, where we read about a cheating tax collector, Zacchaeus, who climbed up a sycamore tree so he could see Jesus going by. Jesus took note of him and said, "Zacchaeus, hurry and come down, for I must stay at your house today" (verse 5).

You'll remember that tax collectors in Jesus' day had a terrible reputation. Let's just say that ninety-nine percent of them gave the other one percent a bad name! While Jesus was at Zacchaeus's house, the latter confessed his wrongdoings and said, "The half of my goods I give to the poor. And if I have defrauded anyone of anything, I restore it fourfold" (verse 8). Jesus then said, "Today salvation has come to this house" (verse 9). The evidence of Zacchaeus's repentance was his commitment to restitution for the wrong he'd done. We don't necessarily have to pay back four or five times the amount, but we should do whatever we can to make a situation right again.

Here's another example: My wife, Rebecca, and I know an older man whom I shall call Bill. He's very wise. He heard about two teenagers from Christian homes who were asked to leave school because of misbehavior and the suspicion that they were into pornography. So Bill, with a redemptive mindset, invited the boys to live in his home.

When they arrived, Bill asked the boys to open their suitcases. They answered, "Well, we can't open the suitcases because we don't know where the key is."

"That's okay," Bill said. "I don't have anything to do. I can sit here while you're looking for the key." A little while later, Bill left the room to answer the telephone. When he returned, behold, the key had been found, and the boys had put all their stuff away. Bill asked, "Okay, boys, where is it?"

"Where is what?" came the sheepish reply.

Bill looked under the bed, and there was a stash of pornography that they had stolen from the local convenience store. So Bill told them, "Here's what we're going to do. We're going to burn this material. But before we do that, we're going to add up the cost of these magazines." (The total was about $250.)

Then Bill gave the boys work they could do in order to earn enough money to repay the cost of the stolen magazines. Within time, they had earned the money. So the three of them went to the convenience store to repay the owner. The boys said, "Here is money to pay for the pornography magazines taken from your back room." The storeowner was smitten in his conscience and Bill asked him, "Do you really want to be corrupting boys like this?" He answered, "No, even my wife told me I shouldn't be selling this stuff. I'm not going to sell it anymore."

That's remarkable enough. But these two young men are now serving God in a Christian ministry. Being willing to pay back what is owed is one way to train our consciences about the seriousness of our offenses.

When it comes to restitution, sometimes money isn't the answer. There are other ways restoration is possible—such as through spending time with a person, or doing positive acts of kindness and sacrifice. In these ways, we are affirming our desire to admit that we were wrong and that we are serious about repairing the damage.

Determine to Change

A fourth way to show sincerity in restoration is to say, "I want to change." This expresses repentance and accountability. I once received a letter in which a woman wrote, "My husband started texting with another woman whom he said he found exciting and smart. I knew nothing about this for months. When I ask him about it, he says it means nothing. But what can I do now that trust has been broken?"

In typical fashion, this man minimized his connection to this other woman whom he found "exciting." He wanted his wife to believe that it was not a big deal. But whenever a marriage partner gives a piece of his or her heart to someone else, it affects the intimacy of the marriage relationship. In this case, it would be right for the wife to insist that there be consequences for her husband's emotional affair, which is almost as hurtful as physical adultery. She could ask that he become accountable to some trusted person, and if not, then she would expose his infraction to a counselor or pastor who would then become involved in the dispute. The bottom line; She needed to make it clear that they can't progress in their marriage relationship until this breach of trust was addressed. And if he doesn't feel her pain, it is impossible for them to be fully restored.

When you wrong another person and trust has been violated, you need to show a determination to change. To ask for forgiveness without intending to change is utterly meaningless. Reconciliation demands that the future be different from the past. Without change, the cycle will simply continue to repeat itself. Before you can move forward, you must commit to a plan for making real change take place.

Ask for Forgiveness

Before reconciliation can take place, it's necessary to ask for forgiveness. When a wrong has been done, you need to say, "Can you find it in your heart to forgive me for what I've done?" Whenever possible, it's very important that the person you've offended be able to say, "Yes, I forgive you." Seeking and extending forgiveness is so important for maintaining relationships.

But maybe the other person won't be able to forgive you. Maybe they'll say, "No, I can't. The hurt is too deep," or "I need more time." Whatever the response, it's still crucial that you seek the forgiveness that you need for reconciliation.

A woman came to me for counsel after her husband ran off and married another woman, leaving her and the children behind. When the children were scheduled to take part in a play at school, the remarried husband wrote to his ex-wife and asked if they could attend this event together to show their support for their children. He wrote, "Why can't we just be friends? Can we go to the play together for the benefit of the kids? I'll be with my new wife, but why can't the three of us all be there? Let the past be past."

His ex-wife asked me to help her write a letter to him. Basically

I suggested she write something like this: "Your ex-wife wants exactly what you do. She also wants to be able to go out and let the past be past, but you can't act as if nothing had happened. She's not going to be there pretending that there's a measure of reconciliation when you haven't said one word of apology. You have destroyed your marriage, put your children through incredible pain, and now, without any repentance or understanding of the hurt you've caused, you just want to pretend that everything is okay and that she should just let bygones be bygones."

Some people who do immeasurable harm to others see their infractions as minor bumps on the road of life. They take the view that the sooner others get over what happened, the sooner everyone can move on. In all this, they act as if no harm was done. In this fantasyland, the perpetrator sees himself as completely justified in his actions, and assumes he doesn't need to ask for forgiveness or to acknowledge wrongdoing.

You will always find those who refuse to see their evil as anything more than superficial; they feel no pain except their own. At best, they think saying, "I'm sorry" is enough, but they fail to reconcile the broken promises, the betrayal, and the pain their words and actions have caused.

Applying the Principles

Isn't it wonderful to know that God is a redeeming God? He knows all about us, including the details of our sins, and yet He invites us to come to Him and be forgiven forever. And as we get to know ourselves and our own proclivity to sin, we must exercise the same grace to others that we have been shown in Jesus Christ our Lord.

Once reconciliation with others has been realized and forgiveness has been extended, the past must no longer be brought up and rehashed when a crisis comes into the relationship. Don't recount that which has been forgiven. A man who had committed adultery told me that although his wife said she had forgiven him, whenever they had an argument, she would always "rub his nose" in the dirt of his past.

There's little you can do with anyone who claims to forgive but actually refuses to act on that forgiveness. In a case like that, the offender must simply live with the reality that God has forgiven; God knows and understands. We must do all we can to effect reconciliation and must accept the fact that, for one reason or another, our efforts are not always successful.

Remember, you don't need to feel shame even if there are people who think you should. If you have cleared your conscience before God and others, you need not live in the shadow of other people's perceptions or expectations. Even some of your friends might think that you have no right to happiness because of what you have done. But God thinks differently. David knew that his joy in God would return even though there was nothing he could do to rectify the mess he had made. His family was probably determined to make sure that he never forgot his sin. But his relationship with God was not tied to his family's intentions and perceptions (Psalm 51:12).

Meanwhile, we can rejoice in knowing that God will not "rub our noses in the dirt." In fact, the dirt has been removed from His sight. Your sins might still be on your mind, but they're not on His! He says, "I have blotted out your transgressions like a cloud, and your sins like mist" (Isaiah 44:22).

Gary Chapman tells a sweet story in his book about a time when his little granddaughter came over for a visit. She asked if she could have some stickers, and her grandmother told her, "Yes, you can have any three stickers you want, but only three."

The little girl went to the drawer where the stickers were kept—and soon, stickers began to show up all over the house. So Gary's wife went to their granddaughter and said, "You were told you could take only three stickers. You disobeyed Grandma." The little girl began to cry and said, "I need someone to forgive me."[2]

You and I need someone to forgive us. Thank God that in Jesus Christ, He sent Someone to forgive us and cleanse us from all unrighteousness. Now, with His help, we must learn to forgive others. Let us make sure that the challenges of reconciling with others draws us closer to God and not away from Him.

Sometimes we must risk all, particularly our reputation, to bring about reconciliation. We must say, "For the good of God and my conscience, I will take care of my side of the reconciliation process, no matter what the cost." Maybe you should seek counsel from someone you respect so you can get help as you walk your way through the reconciliation process. Blessed are those who have a conscience free of offense before God and others.

A Passage to Ponder:

Many years ago in our marriage, my wife Rebecca and I agreed we would try to live by this verse. Memorize it and trust God to bring it to your mind often:

Be kind to one another, tenderhearted, forgiving one another as God in Christ forgave you (Ephesians 4:32).

Probing Questions to Consider:

Can you think of a matter that you have confessed to God, but in your heart you know it should also be confessed to the person you have wronged? If you were confronted with the reality of imminent death, who would you want to speak to in order to make things right? Ask God to give you the grace to make such a confession now. If you need guidance, go to a trusted friend or your pastor. How much will being right with God and *others* cost you?

A Clear Conscience:
Engaging a Hostile Culture

Conscience is the voice of the soul.

A Polish proverb

Tragically, most Christians don't witness to others about their faith in Christ. We might think it is because they don't know how to speak about their faith, or perhaps it is because they fear they will not be able to answer objections. We think that if only we taught more courses on how to do evangelism, or trained believers how to answer the opponents of Christianity, then they would be more willing to begin a spiritual conversation.

There is some truth to those observations. But I believe—and at least one survey I've read concurs—that another reason many Christians are silent is because they have a troubled conscience. Because their heart condemns them, they think to themselves, *How can I share the good news of the gospel when I myself am suffering from unconquered sin? My life as a Christian is hardly a model of what others would expect of a person who claims to be a follower of Jesus Christ.*

At times we all have felt that given our past (or present) struggles with recurring sin we are unworthy to share the gospel with anyone. As we listen to the internal voices of condemnation we are reduced to silence, and we find ourselves hoping that someday our experience will catch up with our theology and we will finally be able to share our faith with confidence and integrity.

At the beginning of this book we looked at 1 John 3:21: "Beloved, if our heart does not condemn us, we have confidence before God." A heart that feels condemned cannot have confidence before God. And if we don't have confidence toward God, we cannot witness with a sense of freedom and assurance.

But hopefully this book has made it clear that our conscience does not have the last word. Through Christ there is both cleansing and renewal of our inner lives. Yes, we can live and speak with confidence toward God.

A Good Conscience Frees Us

The apostle Peter makes a connection between a good conscience and our willingness to defend our faith even in the face of persecution. The increasing opposition to Christianity we face in America and other parts of the world is not a new phenomenon. In Peter's day emperor worship was mandatory, but he believed that if people had a clear conscience, they could respectfully withstand the pressure to comply with what culture demanded.

Let's unpack this passage:

> Even if you should suffer for righteousness' sake, you will be blessed. Have no fear of them, nor be troubled, but in your hearts honor Christ the Lord as holy, always being prepared to make a defense to anyone who asks you for a reason for the hope that is in you; yet do it with gladness and respect, *having a good conscience*, so that when you are slandered, those who revile your good behavior in Christ may be put to shame. For it is better to suffer for doing good, if that should be God's will, than for doing evil (1 Peter 3:14-17, emphasis added).

Consider what Peter is saying.

First, he assumes that believers will live differently than those in the world around them. The reason, of course, is because they have been redeemed by Christ, given a new nature, and they have determined to keep their conscience clear. Wanting to maintain a good conscience means not wanting to accept or participate in the world's values. So, for example, they will refrain from gossiping at the office or engaging in underhanded activities. They will show care and kindness, and sacrifice of themselves in order to "do good...[and] seek peace and pursue it" (verse 11).

Stuart Briscoe tells the story that when he was a college student, he worked for a bank in England managed by a dishonest man who wanted Stuart to, in effect, cheat their customers. But Stuart told him, "If you want me to steal *for* you, what makes you think I will not steal *from* you?" That's an example of a man who was careful about keeping his conscience clear.

Second, Peter taught that those who have a good conscience will be prepared to "make a defense to anyone who asks for a reason for the hope that is in [them]; yet do it with gentleness and respect" (verse 15). Furthermore, Peter said that the worldly antagonists who reviled believers would be put to shame by the example set by those believers, who lived by a different set of values. God will use our integrity, kindness, and humility to convict the world. In Peter's words, "Those who revile your good behavior in Christ will be put to shame" (verse 16).

A good conscience gives us the freedom to do what is right despite the pressures and expectations of a culture that has turned against God.

A New Beginning

Perhaps you've had times when you didn't share your faith because you felt the inner voice of guilt and knew that you were not representing Christ very well. By staying silent, you may have thought you were doing the Lord a favor. You did not want to tarnish His reputation by telling others that you were one of His followers while, at the same time, you lived in the shadow of a condemning conscience.

My prayer is that because of what you have learned from this book, you are no longer listening to those voices that seek to condemn you. If your conscience has been nagging you and keeping you silent, I pray that you will now live without slipping back into past behavioral ruts and become a better witness to the saving work of Christ.

If you have failed others in the past, talk to them one-on-one and ask their forgiveness. Admit that, as a follower of Christ, you have not represented the Lord as well as you should have. Humbly confess that you are a struggling Christian, but a Christian nonetheless. Then share your testimony. People hate hypocrisy, but they welcome honesty from anyone who has failed and is willing to admit it.

I believe that as representatives of Christ, we have a great opportunity to impact our culture, and more importantly, change the spiritual direction of those who are within our sphere of influence. Think of the privilege of living at a time when we have millions of seekers trying to find their way amid a blizzard of religious options. Many people are seeking fulfillment, and we have the privilege of pointing them in the right direction on their spiritual journey. Remember, many people live their entire lives trying to stifle the voice of their conscience. As a believer, you hold the answer so people can have a clear conscience.

I'm convinced that if large numbers of people turn to God, it won't be because of major evangelistic campaigns, or because we have made clever use of the Internet or religious movies or TV programs. If we see a major revival of Christianity, it will be because individual believers stepped to the plate, shared their faith, and lived out the gospel in their homes, neighborhoods, and workplaces—believers like you.

Our present challenge is like that of the early Christians, who lived in a culture driven by a passionate commitment to false religious devotion. Emperor worship, along with the worship of a myriad of gods and goddesses, dominated Roman culture and thought. The pagan populaces were willing to add Jesus to the long list of gods that could be worshiped. What they refused to tolerate was the idea that there was only one true God, and that He said all other rivals were worthless idols. In other words, the pagans said Jesus could be a god, but they were offended by the teaching that He was King of kings and Lord of lords.

Peter would say to us today, "Live with a clear conscience. Have no fear. Defend Christ with gentleness and respect!"

These words are as relevant to us today as they were to believers in the first century AD. Yes, we must challenge the religious climate of our time, but we must do it with humility, respect, and a knowledge that is prepared to give a reason for the hope within us.

So how do we witness to our faith?

Silent No More

A good conscience will allow us to draw a line in the sand even at great personal cost. We will be given the grace to live our convictions, no matter how hard it gets. Not for a moment do I minimize the pressure some people have had to endure in order to maintain their witness. In fact, when we hear stories about what believers face in other countries, we have to ask whether we would be able to weather similar political or religious opposition.

A few years ago, I spoke to a pastor who lives in East Germany. Up till 1989, the area in which he lived was under Soviet control. He told me about how communism had taught Christians to be silent about their beliefs. Those who professed their faith and attended church were marginalized by intimidation and humiliation. A parent might be told, "I understand you attend church. Well, unless you stop attending, your children will not be allowed to attend school, and you will be bypassed for a job promotion." Through such pressure, many Christians became silent. Their faith was privatized and not passed on to the next generation. Sadly, even today, only about thirteen percent of the population attends church.

Peter had these words for those who were being persecuted:

> Beloved, do not be surprised at the fiery trial when it comes upon you to test you, as though something strange were happening to you. But rejoice insofar as you share Christ's sufferings, that you may also rejoice and be glad when his glory is revealed. If you are insulted for the name of Christ, you are blessed, because the Spirit of glory and of God rests upon you...Therefore let those who suffer according to God's will entrust their souls to a faithful Creator while doing good (1 Peter 4:12-14, 19).

When the apostle Paul was defending his ministry, it was his clear conscience that allowed him to witness with boldness: "Our boast is this, *the testimony of our conscience*, that we behaved in the world with simplicity and godly sincerity, not by earthly wisdom but by the grace of God, and supremely so toward you" (2 Corinthians 1:12, emphasis added). Paul's clear conscience was the basis for his boldness. Without his clear conscience, he could not share the gospel with integrity and grace.

Let us agree that we will be silent no more. We must avoid being obnoxious, but at the same time, we should not keep our mouths closed. I've discovered the best way to make it possible to share my faith is by asking questions, by trying to find out where others are on their own spiritual journey. Invite discussion and take time to understand what others are thinking about God, religion, and Jesus in particular.

How is this done? Here are some questions I've used to begin a spiritual conversation:

- Where are you on your spiritual journey?
- How much adult consideration have you given to the Bible?
- What is your perception of God?
- What has been your experience, if any, with Christianity?
- Would you mind if I were to share with you something that someone once shared with me that changed my life?
- I'd love to pray for you. Do you have anything you'd like me to pray about over the next couple of weeks?

Of course you could come up with other kinds of questions. But you never want to give a discourse about Christ without first taking the time to graciously learn about where people are at on their spiritual journey. Do what Jesus did—He frequently began dialogue with others by asking them questions.

Many Christians are intimidated by the prospect of sharing their faith because they are afraid they won't know how to answer people's questions. But in today's religious climate, being a good listener is more important than being a good talker. People want to be heard. And listening to what they say and how they feel is the first step to building a bridge that leads to their hearts.

What if you encounter hostility? Befriend the person so you can learn why he or she is so angry. What is it about Christianity that turns them off? Many people have, humanly speaking, good reason to regard believers with skepticism and distrust. Friendship—true friendship—is still the best means of evangelism. One reason the believers in the early church were so successful at drawing people to Christ is that they practiced the art of hospitality. Their kindness won the attention of those around them.

I've often given a non-Christian friend or colleague a book to read that I think they'll enjoy, and then told them that I'd like to discuss the book with them in the upcoming weeks. The book itself might or might not be gospel-centered; what's important is that the book opens the door to further dialogue. Other books can follow.

Be patient. Be kind. Be honest. Be humble.

Remember that the people of the world fear exposure. They do not want to be confronted with who they really are. As we learned earlier, people will do whatever they can to make themselves look much better than their conscience tells them they are. Our honesty about who we are will give them permission to be honest about who they are. The Holy Spirit works through the conscience to show people their need.

God will not hold us accountable if others do not believe the gospel; rather, He will hold us accountable if we do not share the gospel with others. Our responsibility is to sow the seed. Only He can prepare the soil of the human heart to receive it. Only He can grant the faith needed to believe.

Let our testimony be like that of the apostle Paul:

> Having this ministry by the mercy of God, we do not lose heart. But we have renounced disgraceful, underhanded ways. We refuse to practice cunning or to tamper with God's word, but by the open statement of the truth *we would commend ourselves to everyone's conscience in the sight of God* (2 Corinthians 4:2, emphasis added).

The aim of our charge is love that issues from a pure heart and *a good conscience* and a sincere faith (1 Timothy 1:5, emphasis added).

As God has given us a clear conscience, so we now are free to share the good news that there is more grace in God's heart than sin in our past. As one satisfied customer to another, we point beyond ourselves to the One who graciously and lovingly leads us in our journey toward wholeness.

A Passage to Ponder:

If you should suffer for righteousness' sake, you will be blessed. Have no fear of them, nor be troubled, but in your hearts honor Christ the Lord as holy, always being prepared to make a defense to anyone who asks you for a reason for the hope that is in you; yet do it with gentleness and respect, having a good conscience, so that, when you are slandered, those who revile your good behavior in Christ may be put to shame. For it is better to suffer for doing good, if that should be God's will, than for doing evil (1 Peter 3:14-17).

Probing Questions to Consider:

What is your greatest challenge in witnessing to the power of the gospel?

Can you think of instances when your troubled conscience held you back from telling others about God's forgiveness and grace? Are you willing to pinpoint the reason for your hesitancy and ask God to deal with this part of your life? Are you now determined that you will keep your conscience clear by keeping "current accounts" with God and others?

Notes

Chapter 1—Out of the Shadows

1. Karl Menninger, *Whatever Became of Sin?* (New York: Hawthorn Books, 1973), 14.

2. Albert Camus, *The Fall*, trans. Justin O'Brien (New York: Vintage, 1991), 81.

3. Tim Townsend, *Mission at Nuremberg* (New York: HarperCollins, 2014). This fascinating story of Pastor Gerecke should be read by those who doubt God's ability to save even the vilest offenders.

Chapter 2—It's Not All Your Fault

1. John Piper, "The Key to Experiencing Christmas Peace in Your Life Today," December 25, 2015, http://www.desiringgod.org/interviews/the-keys-to-experiencing-christmas-peace-in-your-life-today.

2. Rodney Clapp, "Shame Crucified, *Christianity Today*, March 11, 1991, 28.

3. "It is Well with My Soul," Horatio Spafford, 1876.

Chapter 3—The Voice of God or the Voice of the Devil

1. C.H. Spurgeon, "Grace Abounding," a sermon preached March 22, 1863, see at https://answersingenesis.org/education/spurgeon-sermons/501-grace-abounding/.

Chapter 4—No Condemnation: No Need for Suicide

1. Charles Swindoll, "Getting Past Guilt: Overcoming Barriers to Feeling Forgiven," June 15, 2009, http://insight.org/resources/article-library/individual/getting-past-guilt-overcoming-barriers-to-feeling-forgiven.

2. William Shakespeare, *Macbeth*, Act 5, Scene 1, 2-3.

3. William G. Justice, *Guilt and Forgiveness* (Grand Rapids: Baker, 1980), 95.

Chapter 5—The Truth That Hurts and Heals

1. Sharon Hersh, *The Last Addiction* (Colorado Springs: WaterBrook, 2008), 13.

2. Mike Wilkerson, *Redemption: Freed by Jesus from the Idols We Worship and the Wounds We Carry* (Wheaton: Crossway, 2011), 169.

3. Quoted in Roland Bainton, *The Reformation of the Sixteenth Century* (Boston: The Beacon Press, 1952), 159.

4. Hersh, *The Last Addiction*, 13.

Chapter 6—The Healing Power of Light

1. Martin Buber, *Good and Evil* (New York: Scribner's, 1953), 111.

2. James Masterson, as quoted by Brennan Manning in *Abba's Child* (Colorado Springs: NavPress, 1994), 27.

3. Barbara Finand, as quoted by Manning, *Abba's Child*, 74.

4. John Claypool, as told to Ken Hyatt, "Freedom Behind Bars," *The Standard*, April 1999, 22-23.

5. Robert Fulghum, *All I Really Needed to Know I Learned in Kindergarten: Uncommon Thoughts on Common Things* (New York: Villard Books, 1988), 56-58.

Chapter 8—Becoming That Impossible Person

1. See at https://www.bpdcentral.com/faq/personality-disorders.

Chapter 9—Forever Forgiven

1. "Alas! And Did My Savior Bleed?" by Isaac Watts (1707).

2. Augustus Toplady, "A Debtor to Mercy Alone," 1771.

Chapter 10—When Sorry Isn't Enough

1. Gary Chapman and Jennifer Thomas, *When Sorry Isn't Enough* (Chicago: Northfield, 2013).

2. Chapman and Thomas, *When Sorry Isn't Enough*, 150.

Other Harvest House Books
by Erwin W. Lutzer

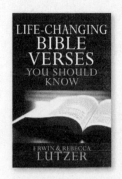

Life-Changing Bible Verses You Should Know

Do you desire to experience the life-changing power of God's Word? Do you long to hide God's Word in your heart, but don't know where to start?

In this book, Bible teacher Erwin Lutzer and his wife, Rebecca, have carefully selected more than 100 Bible verses that speak directly to the most important issues of life, and explained the very practical ways those verses can encourage and strengthen you.

Covering Your Life in Prayer

Every Christian longs for a better and more intimate prayer life. And one of the most effective ways you can grow more powerful in prayer is to learn from the prayers of others. In this book you'll discover new ways to pray—new requests, concerns, and thanksgivings you can bring to God's throne of grace. A wonderful resource for expanding your prayer horizons and enriching your relationship with God.

The Cross in the Shadow of the Crescent

Islam is on the rise all over the West, including in America. In this compelling book, Erwin Lutzer urges Christians to see this as both an opportunity to share the gospel and a reason for concern. Along the way, you'll find helpful answers to these questions and more:

- How does Islam's growing influence affect me personally?
- In what ways are our freedoms of speech and religion in danger?
- How can I extend Christ's love to Muslims around me?

A sensitive, responsible, and highly informative must-read!